MW00988372

The NOTEBOOK
of TRIGORIN

BY TENNESSEE WILLIAMS

PLAYS

Baby Doll & Tiger Tail
Camino Real
Cat on a Hot Tin Roof
Clothes for a Summer Hotel
Dragon Country
The Glass Menagerie
A Lovely Sunday for Creve Coeur
The Red Devil Battery Sign
Small Craft Warnings
Something Cloudy, Something Clear
Stopped Rocking and Other Screen Plays
A Streetcar Named Desire
Sweet Bird of Youth
THE THEATRE OF TENNESSEE WILLIAMS, VOLUME I
   Battle of Angels, A Streetcar Named Desire, The Glass Menagerie
THE THEATRE OF TENNESSEE WILLIAMS, VOLUME II
   The Eccentricities of a Nightingale, Summer and Smoke, The Rose
   Tattoo, Camino Real
THE THEATRE OF TENNESSEE WILLIAMS, VOLUME III
   Cat on a Hot Tin Roof, Orpheus Descending, Suddenly Last Summer
THE THEATRE OF TENNESSEE WILLIAMS, VOLUME IV
   Sweet Bird of Youth, Period of Adjustment, The Night of the Iguana
THE THEATRE OF TENNESSEE WILLIAMS, VOLUME V
   The Milk Train Doesn't Stop Here Anymore, Kingdom of Earth (The Seven Descents
   of Myrtle), Small Craft Warnings, The Two-Character Play
THE THEATRE OF TENNESSEE WILLIAMS, VOLUME VI
   27 Wagons Full of Cotton and Other Short Plays
THE THEATRE OF TENNESSEE WILLIAMS, VOLUME VII
   In the Bar of a Tokyo Hotel and Other Plays
THE THEATRE OF TENNESSEE WILLIAMS, VOLUME VIII
   Vieux Carré, A Lovely Sunday for Creve Coeur, Clothes for a Summer
   Hotel, The Red Devil Battery Sign
27 Wagons Full of Cotton and Other Plays
The Two-Character Play
Vieux Carré

POETRY

Androgyne, Mon Amour
In the Winter of Cities

PROSE

Collected Stories
Hard Candy and Other Stories
One Arm and Other Stories
The Roman Spring of Mrs. Stone
Where I Live: Selected Essays

Lynn Redgrave as Madame Arkadina in the Cincinnati Playhouse
in the Park production of *The Notebook of Trigorin*.

Photo © Sandy Underwood; courtesy of the Cincinnati Playhouse in the Park.

TENNESSEE WILLIAMS

The NOTEBOOK *of* TRIGORIN

A FREE ADAPTATION OF
ANTON CHEKHOV'S
The Sea Gull

BASED ON A TRANSLATION
FROM THE RUSSIAN BY
ANN DUNNIGAN

EDITED, WITH AN
INTRODUCTION, BY
ALLEAN HALE

A NEW DIRECTIONS BOOK

The Notebook of Trigorin is published by arrangement with The University of the South, Sewanee, Tennessee.

Special thanks are due to Thomas Keith for his help in preparing the manuscript.

Manufactured in the United States of America
New Directions Books are printed on acid-free paper.
First published clothbound and as New Directions Paperbook 850 in 1997
Published simultaneously in Canada by Penguin Books Canada Limited

Library of Congress Cataloging-in-Publication Data

Williams, Tennessee. 1911–1983.
   The notebook of Trigorin : a free adaptation of Anton Chekhov's the sea gull / Tennessee Williams; edited, with an introduction by Allean Hale.
     p. cm.
   "Based on a translation from the Russian by Ann Dunnigan."
   ISBN 0-8112-1371-4 (cloth). — ISBN 0-8112-1362-5 (pbk.)
   I. Hale, Allean, 1914–   . II. Chekhov, Anton Pavlovich.
   1860–1904. Chalka. III. Title.
PS3545.I5365N68 1997
812'.54—dc21   97-25480
                                                     CIP

New Directions books are published for James Laughlin
by New Directions Publishing Corporation,
80 Eighth Avenue, New York 10011

TABLE OF CONTENTS

INTRODUCTION:
TWO MASTERS, ONE PLAY

The Notebook of Trigorin is the realization of Tennessee Williams' lifelong dream to interpret *The Sea Gull*, which he called "the first and greatest modern play." Williams was twenty-four and still "Tom" when he discovered Chekhov. He had just had a nervous breakdown, brought on by typing orders eight hours a day in a shoe factory and writing all night. Recovering at his grandparents' in Memphis in the summer of 1935, he first read Chekhov in the library of nearby Rhodes College. Instantly attracted to the stories, he went on to read the letters and plays and felt in Chekhov's life an affinity with his own. He saw his household as if it were a Chekhov drama: a group of unhappy people bound to each other by circumstance and blood, living out their daily routine in frustration. Chekhov's portraits of an aristocratic culture giving way to a bourgeois society seemed akin to his own family's experience: the genteel mother and grandparents, forced from a rural idyllic South to the confines of industrial St. Louis.

When Tom entered Washington University that fall, he studied playwriting. He kept a framed picture of the Russian playwright above his typewriter and for his assignment in a literature class wrote an enthusiastic essay: "Birth of an Art (Anton Chekhov and The New Theatre)." His strict Germanic professor marked on it, "No page numbers! . . . This in no way fulfills the requirement of a term paper. . . ." Williams, like Chekhov's Constantine, would always ignore the rules. Actually, his twenty-two page paper was discerning, reviewing the social background of Chekhov's work, tracing his history as a playwright and commenting on his theatrical innovations. He compared Chekhov to Ibsen, Shaw, and O'Neill, pointing out that whereas lyricism permeated a Chekhov play, when O'Neill's characters become lyrical "one suspects them of having had a few drinks. . . ." He noted that *The Sea Gull* is "a tragedy of inaction" and that although perhaps fifty per cent of the speeches would seem to have no direct bearing on the story, actually "every line belongs in its place."

Williams especially identified with Constantine, the young playwright in *The Sea Gull*. Tom's early journals record the same self-doubt and romantic anguish which Constantine suffers; like him, the young Williams was shy, sensitive, passionate, often in depair, even contemplating suicide. Each had an ambivalent relationship with a domineering mother. In the back of a college textbook he had scrawled a line from Strindberg: "It is called love-hatred and it hails from the pit." Constantine's passionate cry for new forms in the theatre sounds very much like Williams' plea for "a plastic theatre" which would involve music, dance, and the visual arts. In a youthful journal [1943] he wrote that realistic drama was dead. The play of the future would be a series of short cumulative scenes. Actors would perform on one simple set where a pillar could represent a building, a chandelier a drawing room; exterior could be transformed to interior by lighting. "The straight realistic play with its genuine frigidaire and its authentic ice-cubes, its characters that speak exactly as its audience speaks" must give way to a drama of psychological action.

Williams' staging innovations, realized in *The Glass Menagerie* a year later, were to change American theatre. The first reviews of that play noted its "Chekhovian" mood, a description that would be repeated by critics from *Summer and Smoke* to *Night of the Iguana*. Williams had already established the link in a 1941 one-act, *The Lady of Larkspur Lotion*, where his Writer, asked his name, cries out "Chekhov! Anton Pavlovich Chekhov!" Most of his one-act plays resemble Chekhov stories, brief inconclusive glimpses into a character's life at some telling moment. He had Chekhov's same feeling for human isolation and the impossibility of people understanding each other.

Like Chekhov, Williams was as much poet as playwright. He was especially drawn to *The Sea Gull,* which he called "my favorite of all plays." Its characters, two playwrights and two actresses, attracted him immediately, and its theme of the artist's struggles against society's indifference fit his own experience at the time. By eerie coincidence, Tennessee's first professional production, the 1940 *Battle of Angels,* ended in a debacle of smoke and fumes, driving out the audience, exactly as did the sulfurous fumes in Constantine's dream play. In *Battle,* Val's poetic monologue about the legless bird which can never come to earth is reminiscent of *The Sea Gull* in both subject and style. Arkadina derides Nina's long opening speech as a "recitative." Almost every Williams drama has such monologues—lyrical "arias." One might speculate that *The Sea Gull* influenced *A Streetcar Named Desire;* in both, people's lives are being destroyed during a game of cards. Stanley's final line, "This game is seven card stud," echoes Trigorin's triumphal "The game is mine!"

Even after *Streetcar* in 1947 established Williams as a leading American playwright, he thought of Chekhov and *The Sea Gull.* Three years later, learning that his friend Paul Bigelow might produce the play he begged to collaborate on the staging. "It would be a thrilling experience to help bring a play like that into its difficult, very delicate sort of reality," he wrote. The project fell through, but in 1953 he wrote critic Brooks Atkinson that his dream now was to direct *The Sea Gull.* He would cast Brando as Constantine, Stella Adler as Mme. Arkadina, Geraldine Page as Nina. Through the years when interviewers asked which three writers had influenced him the most, he answered "Chekhov! Chekhov! Chekhov!"

In the seventies, writing his *Memoirs,* he was reminded of his ambition to reinterpret Chekhov's play. While he still loved the poetry of the writing, he now felt that it held too much in reserve, that it had never been let out of the confines of the translation "straitjacket." At different periods he had empathized with various characters in *The Sea Gull*; in his youth with Constantine, the idealistic experimentor; in middle age with Dr. Dorn, the detached bystander who observes the other characters and has them face their reality. Now he saw himself in Trigorin, the world-weary writer. Williams, too, had made compromises with the demands of success.

It was only near the end of his life and outside his own country that his dream of interpreting *The Sea Gull* was realized. In 1980 he was invited to the University of British Columbia in Vancouver to conduct writing seminars. The added incentive was that *The Red Devil Battery Sign*, a late play he was revising, would be produced by the Vancouver Playhouse. In the last decade Williams' work had been better received abroad than in the United States. Here his audience expected more big dramas like *Streetcar* or *Cat on a Hot Tin Roof*, whereas he now wanted to experiment with new forms. Working with the Playhouse director, Roger Hodgman, he mentioned his lifelong ambition to adapt *The Sea Gull* and was commissioned to prepare his own version to be the season's opener in September 1981. Through the summer he wrote Hodgman enthusiastic reports. He thought that much in the play was so understated that it was not understood by today's public. His intent was to make what was whispered in Chekhov, speak out boldly. He would try to give a more contemporary treatment, more theatrical excitement. Whether he succeeded or failed, his effort must be seen as an act of love. He informed Hodgman that he was working from two translations, Ann Dunnigan's, which he called "the best," and Stark Young's, citing Constance Garnett's early standard translation as stilted and "downright illiterate." It is a surprise to find Williams, so often derided by critics as non-intellectual, engaged in the scholarly work of comparing translations. To see the master playwright of one generation humbly pondering the working methods of the earlier master is somehow touching and provides a glimpse of how each one created. Looking back on fifty years of playwriting, he could trace his own progression from idealistic to practical; in that lifetime he had learned that even the most significant ideas must be translated into the popular language of the theatre.

Williams approached his project with some trepidation. His Russian friend Maria St. Just was so outraged that he would take liberties with the sacred play that she hid his book. He knew others would share her feeling that to make any textual changes would be taking license. But he had always taken risks. He already had in mind a different ending—instead of Chekhov's narrated last line, action that would involve visual magic. He called his version *The Notebook of Trigorin*, taking the title from "The Notebook of Anton Chekhov" which he had read so long ago. However, by mid-June he had sent Hodgman only bits and pieces of writing. Now, less than two years before his death, Williams' energy was depleted. He had had no critical success since *Night of the Iguana*, in 1961; his final play to be shown on Broadway, *Clothes for a Summer Hotel*, 1980, was a failure. Between his deteriorating health, his constant travels, demands from the Goodman Theatre in Chicago for their spring, 1981, production of his last long play, *A House Not Meant to Stand*, and from New York where *Something Cloudy, Something Clear* would be performed that August, his new script had not materialized. The Vancouver rehearsals for *The Notebook of Trigorin* began that same month with no Williams and no adaptation. They had to start with Chekhov's original, using a set which bore little relation to either playwright's concept. When the wayward author did show up, his script changes alarmed the cast. He had brought Chekhov's buried conflicts to the surface; his submerged melodrama was acted out in an ending where Arkadina must finally face her part in her son's tragedy. The play ran from September 12 to

October 10, but there was resentment about the playwright's early defection. After he left, Chekhov's ending was restored.

Williams rewrote his ending after the Canadian production, and continued to revise the play until he died in 1983. The script was lying among other unpublished manuscripts on an agent's desk when an English director, Stephen Hollis, saw it and commenced his fourteen-year effort to have it produced. Maria St. Just, as a trustee of Williams' estate—and perhaps over-zealous to protect his reputation—had denied permission for any production until she could re-evaluate the work under appropriate circumstances. She arranged a successful reading at Lincoln Center on December 14, 1992, with a cast including Marsha Mason, George Grizzard, and Kate Burton, but no production materialized. It was only after her death that Hollis and the Cincinnati Playhouse secured permission for a full-scale stage production. This event in October 1996 celebrated the 100th anniversary of *The Sea Gull's* first performance in 1896 as well as the premiere of the play as Tennessee Williams envisioned it.

What sort of play did the Cincinnati audience see? In general, what Chekhov narrates, Williams demonstrates. He puts onstage what in Chekhov happens offstage. Williams brings more visible craft to the play, and by using the very dramatic devices Chekhov avoided—plot, conflict, action, climax, denouement—makes it more theatrical. Technically, he pays more attention to staging, modernizes period references, adds walk-on or exit lines where needed. At the opening of *The Sea Gull,* the makeshift stage for Constantine's performance is merely noted in the directions and mentioned casually by Masha; Williams shows the business of stagehands erecting it, in effect saying, this is a play about theatre. He makes the play more vigorous by summarizing Chekhov's long philosophical musings, breaking the characters' lines into shorter speeches. While Chekhov's humor is so subtle in translation as to be lost on a modern audience, Williams injects more obvious comedy. What are implications in Chekhov's character portraits, Williams amplifies. Chekhov shows Trigorin dominated by Arkadina with no explanation. Williams invents a scene to explain it. While in Chekhov actions seem to happen incidentally, Williams predicts and prepares, giving clues, building suspense. Where Chekhov's characters behave and talk as in real life, undirected, uttering irrelevancies, Williams manipulates them to advance the plot. Chekhov paints his people in an impressionistic way, whereas Williams is expressionistic, emphasizing their motives and emotions. His probing extends even to the minor characters. His treatment of Masha and Medvedenko illustrate his technique. Their opening dialogue in *The Sea Gull* on the surface tends to make them seem one-dimensional, her a depressive, him a bore. He loves her; she despises him. She serves mainly to furnish the exposition and perform necessary actions. (She makes a bed, draws the curtains, summons Kostya, keeps the card game going.) She is consistently taciturn and bitter. Williams shows that Masha is more complicated. He focuses on Medvedenko's famous line "Why do you always wear black?" to build a scene between them which enacts her revulsion and his sexual frustration, creating some sympathy for the schoolmaster. He cuts Masha's long speeches into one-line quips, making her more sardonic than sour and creates a scene between Masha and her mother, to express her hopeless love for Kostya and Polina's equally hopeless love for Dorn.

Williams' Dr. Dorn is also an interesting transformation. Chekhov's Dorn is the logical observer, the realist who comments on the behavior of those around him but feels that it will not change. He perhaps represents the clinical Chekhov who was himself a doctor. He also resembles the detached observer side of Tennessee Williams. (Williams had originally hoped to play the Doctor in the Vancouver production.) Williams changes him from bystander to participant, seizing on

Chekhov's clues. Dorn mentions his success with women-patients; Williams makes him a womanizer, adding comedy to the play as he flirts with each female in turn. Noticing the streak of cruelty in Dorn's indifference, he builds on it. This adds more dramatic contrast, especially in a contrapuntal scene with Arkadina where his sly cynicism further exposes her egotism. If this Dorn seems a departure from Chekhov, it was one of the most effective in the Cincinnati production—an adaptation that obviously "worked."

But Williams' most radical change in the script is his treatment of Trigorin, the writer. Chekhov brings him onstage with notebook in hand, but Williams goes further to make the notebook the play's dominant symbol rather than the sea gull. Whereas Chekhov's Trigorin appears to be genuinely attracted to Nina (though he callously discards her in the end), Williams uncovers his true motivation: "It could be the most important romance I've ever *written*," he has Trigorin cry. This becomes a crucial line in the play, exposing that, for the writer the most sacred emotional experience becomes a paragraph in the ever-present notebook. Williams makes Trigorin the lead character, bringing him center stage, doubling his speeches, having him propel the action, as his relationship with his mistress Arkadina becomes a duel, erupting in the quarrel which is the melodramatic climax of the play. Chekhov presents Trigorin's slavish domination by Arkadina without explanation. He simply admits that he is "soft," "submissive." Williams uses this supposition of traditional "feminine" qualities to make him a bisexual. In a revealing departure from Chekhov's text in Act Two, Williams personalizes Trigorin's long soliloquy on the writer's life to express his own convictions: the writer must recognize both his feminine and masculine sides. This is Williams unmasked, taking his stand against homophobia. For Williams, who sat down at his typwriter every day of his life, Trigorin's obsession with writing, his self-doubts as to its value, his confession that he uses others as material, are his own laments. It is the seventy-year-old playwright who adds: "You live from one work to the next, haunted always by—am I finished? Will there be another?"

Making Trigorin, rather than Constantine, protagonist in the play also moves the spotlight from Nina to Arkadina. Chekhov's Arkadina is chiefly a portrait-of-the-actress, on the surface charming, temperamental, amusing in her egoism. Williams' treatment is an extreme, but logical extension. He pictures her as older, with her career on the wane. Underneath the comedy we feel her desperation. He demonstrates how her self-absorption destroys her son as it has Trigorin. She becomes one of Williams' great "monster woman" characters—a role which in Cincinnati Lynn Redgrave played to the hilt. Arkadina, clutching at past glories, recalls the Princess in *Sweet Bird of Youth;* each has a key speech in defense of theatre. Since Williams so often used his own family as subjects, it is tempting to see in Arkadina a portrait of his mother, who had the same attention to dress, had aspired to be an actress, and who made her quarrels with her husband into dramatic scenes. Arkadina's stinginess, her belittling of her son's writing, might remind him of his father's meanness and how it had affected his youth.

Perhaps Nina, beautiful and doomed, recalled his sister Rose as well. If so, he took the writer's privilege of correcting real life—Chekhov's portrayal of real life—by making Nina stronger. He deletes her incipient "mad scene"—"I am a sea gull. . . ," and adds vigor by substituting short speeches for lengthy monologues. When she returns for a last meeting with Constantine, she summarizes their lives in Williams' words: "Well, so it's gone—our youth." He makes her less effusively romantic and deletes her lofty soliloquy about "having faith" and "bearing one's cross" to focus on having "the strength to endure," his own credo. Building on Chekhov's mention of "a letter from America," he lets Nina's baby live to be adopted in the United States, thus creating a link between the old world and the new—and by implication linking the Russian playwright and the American. Williams is true to Chekhov's symbolism in Nina, her connection with the lake, her virginal white. He sees her as a transcendent figure, like his own Hannah in *Night of the Iguana* who understands the road she must take. It may be more than coincidence that both the names "Nina" and "Hannah" mean "grace."

Finally, the play under Williams' touch becomes more oedipal, uncovering what Chekhov kept underneath. In his college essay on *The Sea Gull,* Tom had noticed the oedipal hint. In writing his adaption, Williams restudied it. Chekhov called his *Sea Gull* a comedy but deliberately built it on a framework of *Hamlet,* the prototypical tragedy. He used the same basic situation of love, hate and jealousy; the same triangle of son, mother, lover; the self-analyzing youth and the discarded young girl, who like Ophelia is associated with flowers and water images. As in Shakespeare's tragedy, there is a play-within-the-play, and the closet scene between Hamlet and Gertrude is imitated when Arkadina binds up Constantine's wounds. Chekhov suggests the connection early in the play by having mother and son greet each other with quotations from *Hamlet.* Williams' technique is to prepare for this opening by having Masha first mention both Hamlet and Ophelia. If Chekhov used the *Hamlet* references subliminally to create a tension which his delicate play eschews, Williams builds on that tension with stylistic changes which are certainly more Shakespeare than Chekhov. One could say that in *The Notebook of Trigorin,* three playwrights are at work. Chekhov, having led his audience to expect the noble demise of Shakespeare's hero, ends with irony: one flat line, "Kostya has shot himself." Shakespeare might have preferred Williams' *coup de théâtre.* Even as her son's body is being borne onstage, Arkadina turns to the audience and gives her final bow—a demonstration that, for a professional, the show must go on.

The Cincinnati Playhouse production was widely and favorably reviewed, with universal agreement on the acting as excellent. A significant factor in its success was the exceptionally beautiful setting by Ming Cho Lee, one of America's foremost designers, who had done previous sets for Williams plays. This was inspired by a black-and-white photograph he had taken of the grounds of Olana, the estate of the nineteenth-century painter Frederick Church in the Hudson River Valley. A subtle, moody scene of water, trees and sky, it reminded him of *The Sea Gull.* For *Trigorin,* the photgraph was transferred to canvas, enlarged to fill the entire backdrop and side walls and even extended onto the stage, so that the reflection of the lake stretched across the floor. This suggested the Russian interpretation of the lake as having magic powers and underscored Chekhov's "when the lake is disturbed, it seems to affect us all." Magical was the evocative lighting by Brian Nason, with its range of color effects, from twilight to thunderstorm. Aside from wicker garden chairs, a table or two, merely the suggestion of doors, the mural was the setting, reinforcing the lyrical quality of the writing and becoming almost a character in the play. Thus the set answered Constantine's plea for "something new"—as well as Williams' manifesto against stage realism.

His hope, to "try to make the script, as I interpret it, so beautiful that it will disarm [critics]" was on the whole successful. "Fascinating," "compelling," "a winner," "humorous," "relevant," "poetic," "an exciting new look at a classic," were some of the comments; Chekhov's and Williams' "ironic wit and abiding compassion for humanity blend well. . . ." One person did observe that the characters seem driven to their ruin, not trapped as in Chekhov. Of twenty reviews only three were negative. Construing Trigorin as a bisexual drew the most controversy: one critic wrote that it would make Chekhov spin in his grave, while another found it "a totally valid interpretation of the role." All agreed that Lynn Redgrave as the aging actress gave a bravura performance, "rich in emotional colors" but there were contrasting opinions on her final action. Where one declared that "it falls flat," another called it "as powerful a moment as one is likely to find in the theatre."

In 1981 when Williams commenced his "free adaption" of *The Sea Gull* he wrote: "I hope this is understood as . . . a profession of deep love for Chekhov. . . . I will probably take more licenses. . . ." Williams does succeed in making the characters and actions of the play more accessible to a contemporary American audience. But in "taking license," he made the play more Williams than Chekhov. Ultimately the best way to approach this drama is as a newly discovered Tennessee Williams work. *The Notebook of Trigorin* gains power when seen as the personal notebook of Tennessee Williams, valuable for what it tells us about the methods and motivations of America's premier playwright. Perhaps, as critic Felicia Londré suggests, Williams has here invented a new form: part adaptation, part interpretation, the fusion of a classic drama by one master with a contemporary original by another. The "magic" he created is that in *The Notebook of Trigorin,* the voices of two great playwrights a century apart are joined in one work of art.

—Allean Hale

The Notebook of Trigorin was given its United States premiere on September 5, 1996, by the Cincinnati Playhouse in the Park, Cincinnati, Ohio. Its performance commemorated the 100th anniversary of *The Sea Gull*'s opening in 1896 in St. Petersburg, Russia. *Trigorin* was directed by Stephen Hollis; set design was by Ming Cho Lee; costume design by Candice Donnelly; lighting by Brian Nason, and sound by David B. Smith. Production stage manager was Bruce E. Coyle, and stage manager, Suann Pollock. Edward Stern was producing artistic director. The cast, in order of appearance, was as follows:

Semyon Semyonovich MEDVEDENKO, a teacher	JACK CIRILLO
MASHA, Shamrayev's daughter	NATACHA ROI
CONSTANTINE Gavrilovich Treplev, Arkadina's son	TIMOTHY ALTMEYER
YAKOV, a workman	JED DAVIS
Pytor Nikolayevich SORIN, Arkadina's brother	DONALD CHRISTOPHER
Boris Alekseyevich TRIGORIN, a writer	JEFF WOODMAN
NINA Mikhailovna Zarechnaya, daughter of a wealthy landowner	STINA NIELSEN
POLINA Andreyevna, Shamrayev's wife	SONJA LANZENER
Yevgeny DORN, a doctor	PHILIP PLEASANTS
Ilya Afanasyevich SHAMRAYEV, Sorin's estate manager	ALAN MIXON
Irina Nikolayevna ARKADINA, an actress	LYNN REDGRAVE
Cook	JOHN SHARP
Old Woman	ELEANOR B. SHEPHERD
Maid	POPPI KRAMER
Workers	JACK MARSHALL
	BRUCE PILKENTON

Grateful acknowledgment is due the Cincinnati Playhouse in whose playbill portions of Allean Hale's Introduction first appeared. We wish to thank especially Edward Stern, Executive Director Buzz Ward, Public Relations Director Peter M. Robinson and Bruce Coyle for preparing and making available the prompt script on which this edition is based; also Publications Manager John P. Bruggen for production photographs and reviews. Stephen Hollis was most helpful in sharing his insights on performance and staging.

Chekhov was a quiet and delicate writer whose huge power was always held in restraint. I know that in a way this may disqualify me as "interpreter" of this first and greatest of modern plays. If I have failed him, it was despite an intense longing to somehow utilize my quite different qualities as a playwright to bring him more closely, more audibly to you than I've seen him brought to you in any American production.

Our theatre has to cry out to be heard at all . . .

—Tennessee Williams

The NOTEBOOK
of TRIGORIN

The play opens by the lake in a section of the park on Sorin's estate. In the foreground a makeshift stage, hurriedly put together, blocks the view. There are bushes left and right of the stage. There are a few chairs and a small table. The sun has just set.

Yakov and other workmen are on the stage behind the curtain; sounds of coughing and hammering are heard. Masha and Medvedenko enter, returning from a walk.

MEDVEDENKO: Masha, tell me; why do you always wear black?

[*She is obviously inattentive to him.*]

You've got no reason to be depressed. You're in good health. Your father's well-off. [*He takes her hand.*]

MASHA: Don't, please don't. I'm touched by your feeling for me but I just can't return it, that's all.

MEDVEDENKO: If I were not so wretchedly poor, twenty-three rubles a month!

MASHA: It isn't a question of money. I could love a beggar if . . .

MEDVEDENKO: The beggar was Constantine. Isn't that so?

MASHA: His mother treats him as one—loves him? —Oh, yes, but love can be cruel as hate. She will despise his play this evening and make no secret of it and she'll be coldly polite, polite as ice to Nina, you'll see. It will be clear that she's what she believes she is, the star that's the greatest in Russia. She probably thinks she's the greatest star of the world.

MEDVEDENKO: Twenty-three rubles a month is what I get.

MASHA: I think you said that.

MEDVEDENKO: Out of that twenty-three rubles, something deducted for the pension fund.

MASHA: How you do go on about money, money, and so loudly.

MEDVEDENKO: Support a witch of a mother.

MASHA: Send her away on a broomstick.

MEDVEDENKO: Two sisters, on my hands for good since they're homely as heifers.

MASHA: Then put them in a pasture.

MEDVEDENKO: My little brother—impossible to control.

MASHA: Semyon, I think that boy would spit in the eye of the infant Jesus.

MEDVEDENKO: That he would. [*He sighs deeply.*] Still, people have to eat and drink.

MASHA: Eat, no, drink, yes. Look, you poor stupid man, you've got this appalling family on your hands and you want me with them, too? This very curious proposal of yours would not be wise to accept, sorry, but—no, Semyon.

MEDVEDENKO: Four miles here, four miles back! —And nothing but rejection from you ever. Oh, I—

[*Constantine steps out before the curtain: Masha involuntarily rises from the bench.*]

CONSTANTINE: Quiet, please, I have to give the stage-hands instructions. They've not put up— [*He turns toward them, behind the curtain.*] —Nina is not able to jump onto the platform like a grasshopper.

YAKOV [*offstage*]: We thought this ladder would—

CONSTANTINE: Somebody hold it for her and help her up it, then! She's going to be late getting here and very nervous because my mother's literary celebrity has condescended to attend.

SASHA: Don't worry. It's for just one performance.

MASHA [*crying out*]: It will have many performances! Not just here tonight, but—

CONSTANTINE: She must not fall! Nail the ladder! To the back of the platform! Not the *side*, she mustn't be seen before the curtain's lifted.

[*Sorin appears upstage, leaning on a cane.*]

SORIN: Kostya . . .

CONSTANTINE: Uncle Petrusha, don't move, there's a slope down.

SORIN: Yes, a long slope down . . . the name of it is age.

CONSTANTINE: Stay there, I'll come fetch you, Uncle. —What was that you were shouting at me, Masha?

MASHA: That I—that I know that— [*She can't continue.*] Excuse me—my opinion—is that it will be played all over Russia, not only one night by this lake! [*Her voice shakes with feeling.*]

CONSTANTINE: Masha, have you been drinking?

SORIN: Kostya!

[*Constantine rushes up to help Sorin. Sorin descends the slope with Constantine's help.*]

Can't be myself in the country, will never accustom myself to life here which isn't what I call life. Want to sleep it away, yes, keep falling asleep. Wake up? —Why? For what? —I dream of life in the city—all I dream of, Kostya. Please! When you leave here—I know you will—please don't leave me alone here.

CONSTANTINE: Be patient. We'll find a way. Just one moment. [*He helps Sorin to a seat.*]

MASHA: They've stopped that infernal hammering on the stage so the performance ought to start soon. Oh, I do hope that Kostya's mother and her—how does one refer to her writer companion?

MEDVEDENKO: His name is Boris Alekseyevich Tri—

MASHA: I know his name. I meant their relationship. Is he really her lover or just a traveling companion?

MEDVEDENKO: Don't they sleep in the same room?

MASHA: Mother says not always: In fact less often than not. He's really closer to her son's age than hers.

MEDVEDENKO: What is her age?

MASHA: Considerably more than you'd guess from her appearance, but her scrapbook shows her appearing as Ophelia before Kostya was born.

MEDVEDENKO: Ophelia is—?

MASHA: *Was!*—a girl in love with Hamlet. [*She dips snuff.*] Do you know who Hamlet was?

[*Medvedenko appears disconcerted.*]

Well? Do you or don't you?

MEDVEDENKO: Naturally. An English actor, but, Masha, Masha, they'll be coming here soon and—you know for a long time now I've tried to find the right occasion, the privacy, the moment, to—

MASHA: I know and I've avoided it.

MEDVEDENKO: You mean—?

MASHA: I could use a cognac. Semyon, bring me a cognac, in a teacup.

[*He trudges off left, in a doleful way.*]

SORIN: I don't feel myself in the country and I never will.

CONSTANTINE: Uncle Petrusha, we'll go to a city, to—

SORIN: Who would take me? Certainly not Irina. Introduce me as her brother, at my age and in my state of—in my condition?

CONSTANTINE: I will—soon as my writing earns me a bit of money. [*He catches sight of Masha.*] Masha, when the play begins we'll call you. Sorry, but for some reason . . .

MASHA: Naturally, I understand, but it will be beautiful, Kostya, I can hardly wait. [*She has started toward the house.*]

SORIN: Maria Ilyinichna, ask your papa to let the dog off its chain so it won't howl all night, and keep everybody awake.

MASHA: Of course, but will he listen? [*She continues to exit off left.*]

SORIN: I tell you that man's begun to behave as if he owns the estate. And you know why? He observes my failing health. So the dog will howl, I'll not sleep— I've never lived as I've wanted to in the country. Once I used to take a month's leave and come here to rest. But as soon as I got here, they began to pester me with all sorts of nonsense, so that by the next day I was ready to leave. Kostya, I was not welcome, not in my own home. I wanted to leave the next day.

YAKOV: We're going for a swim. Sasha!

IVAN: Sasha!

CONSTANTINE: The stage is ready?

YAKOV AND IVAN: Yes! ! !

[*They dash off.*]

CONSTANTINE: Uncle, let me tidy your hair up a bit. [*He combs his uncle's hair. A tenderness between them should be apparent.*] Your beard needs trimming. I'll take care of that to-morrow.

SORIN: Even when I was young I used to look as if I'd been drinking for days.

CONSTANTINE: And nights?

SORIN: Had no luck with the ladies. I feel that even my sis-ter—I know that she's embarrassed by my looks: once she in-troduced me as her grandfather!

CONSTANTINE: Tonight she's going to witness theatre in a new form and I doubt that she'll like it. Jealous. And stingy? I hap-pen to know she's got seventy thousand rubles banked in Odessa—ask her for the price of a decent suit—"My dear boy, don't you know that I have to purchase my own costumes even at the Imperial Theatre because the dress designer provides me with dresses a dog wouldn't wear?"

SORIN: In spite of it all you know your mother loves you . . .

CONSTANTINE [*pulling the petals off a flower*]: She loves me, she loves me not, she— My mother wants a brilliant life for herself only, love for herself only, and I exist for her only as a constant reminder that she has a twenty-five year old son. When I'm not there she's only thirty-two. When I'm there, she's forty-three. Besides, nothing's important to her but the theatre.

7

SORIN: We can't do without the theatre. Our culture can't do without it, Kostya.

CONSTANTINE: All right, but we need new forms—new forms are necessary.

SORIN: *D'accord, d'accord*—by the way, can you figure out this writer Boris Trigorin? Who never opens his mouth?

[*Trigorin has entered upstage.*]

TRIGORIN: Now, now, that's not so, I'm just such a boring talker you don't listen. —I hear splashing, someone's having a swim. You know I could use one, too. Won't you join me, Kostya?

CONSTANTINE: No, thank you, sir. I'm waiting here for Nina Mikhailovna who's going to perform in a sort of play I've written.

TRIGORIN: Of course, I know, I'm—looking forward to it. I understand it's in a new form . . . good—good, very good.

[*He hears his name called, "Boris!" by Arkadina and turns sadly back to the house.*]

CONSTANTINE: If that's what he really hopes, he'll not be disappointed in that respect. We need new forms. And if we can't have them, then we'd better have nothing. [*He looks at his watch.*]

SORIN: Try to love her, Kostya—despite . . .

CONSTANTINE: I love my mother, you know that. Simply don't understand her attachment to this—

SORIN: Before I got washed up here on the shore of this old lake like a dying fish, Kostya, you know there were two things I wanted to accomplish in life, I mean I wanted them passionately. [*He drops his head in his hands.*] I wanted to get married, that was one. The other was to be a writer. Oh, not an important writer, just a minor writer would do me, a writer occasionally published—I succeeded at neither. I succeeded at nothing.

CONSTANTINE: Uncle.

NINA [*from up left*]: I'm here! I'm here!

CONSTANTINE [*springing up*]: Yes, she's here—it's Nina. I see her white dress. Uncle, I can't live without her.

NINA: I'm not late. I'm not late, am I?

CONSTANTINE: No, no.

NINA: I did try desperately to be on time. I even—this man, a total stranger came by in a carriage. Offered me a ride—it was frightening. He looked at me so oddly—luckily we were nearly here—I jumped out and fell—is my dress ruined?

CONSTANTINE: No, no, no, but—

NINA: I'm so breathless.

CONSTANTINE: *Soyez tranquille, maintenant,* but—

SORIN: Kostya may be too timid to tell you this but I'm not. He loves you, trembles when you're with him.

CONSTANTINE: Uncle Petrusha . . .

NINA: Nonsense, Uncle, he's worried about the reception of his play. [*She gives Sorin a hug.*]

CONSTANTINE [*embarrassed*]: It's time to round up our distinguished little audience. I'll—

SORIN [*rising rheumatically*]: No, you stay right here with your beautiful actress. I'll get them down here, *tout de suite.* [*He goes off singing "The Two Grenadiers" off-key. He pauses to catch his breath.*] Once I was singing like that to the Assistant Prosecutor, a powerful man, he could help my career. Well, he interrupted me with this comment: "You have a strong voice, your excellency. Yes. Strong, but revolting." [*He exits.*]

NINA: Just imagine this. My father's wife has convinced him I ought not to come here. Calls it too Bohemian for me. She of all people calls it too Bohemian for me. [*She pauses shyly.*]

CONSTANTINE: Nina, we're alone.

[*Pause. With a loud intake of breath he kisses her. She smiles sadly.*]

NINA: What kind of tree is that?

CONSTANTINE: That tree is an elm.

NINA: Why is it so dark?

CONSTANTINE: After sundown, comes evening. Evening is darker than day—Nina, don't leave right after the performance—*please* don't, Nina.

NINA: I don't know how I'll get home. But I have to and early, before they come back. My father and his awful wife.

CONSTANTINE: Well, then, I'll come to your house.

NINA: You *know* that's impossible, Kostya.

CONSTANTINE: I'll stand all night in the garden, looking up at your window.

NINA: That's a ridiculous idea. The watchman would see you.

CONSTANTINE: I'll sneak in the garden barefoot.

NINA: Tesor would bark.

CONSTANTINE: Nina?

NINA: Yes?

CONSTANTINE: You know I love you and you know how much.

NINA: Ssh. There's someone coming.

CONSTANTINE: Yakov.

YAKOV: Huh?

CONSTANTINE: It's time to begin. Is the moon rising?

YAKOV: Not quite.

CONSTANTINE: Have you got the methylated spirit? Is the sulfur there? You know when the red eyes appear there's got to be the smell of sulfur. They've got to happen at precisely the same time.

NINA: Oh dear, what if I sneeze? If I sneeze once, I sneeze a dozen times.

CONSTANTINE: You're not going to sneeze. One time or a dozen. Are you still so nervous?

NINA: Yes, very.

CONSTANTINE: Because of Mother?

NINA: Not her. I'm used to her. Trigorin! And trying to perform such a difficult play.

CONSTANTINE: What's difficult about my play?

NINA: No living characters and practically no action.

CONSTANTINE: Oh, you want to race around the platform, tearing at your hair, throwing things about?

NINA: Anything would be better than just sitting there, reciting.

CONSTANTINE: Must I explain to you what I thought you understood? *This! Is a dream play.* The deepest, the most, if not only, meaningful reality is in our dreams.

NINA: My dreams, I don't understand them at all.

CONSTANTINE: The mystery of a dream is its beauty, Nina.

NINA: I'm sure, I'm sure. But I wish there were a love scene in this dream play.

CONSTANTINE: A love scene? With a successfully commonplace writer, I suppose. With Trigorin?

NINA: You're insulting me now. And the writer I most admire. I think I'll walk home.

CONSTANTINE: You'll not do any such thing. Seat yourself on the stage. It's nearly moonrise.

[As they cross toward the stage, he embraces her.]

NINA: Don't, please! I do love you, Kostya, but not in this way.

[They disappear behind the stage. Polina and Dorn enter.]

POLINA: It's getting damp. Are you comfortable?

DORN: No, it's humid, sticky.

POLINA: You're a doctor, but you don't take care of yourself.

[Silence. He hums.]

You were so carried away talking to Irina Nikolayevna. Admit you find her attractive.

DORN: She seems to prefer younger men. Men considerably younger than herself.

POLINA: You're still good-looking, Yevgeny, and women like you. It's apparent.

DORN: So what do you want me to do?

POLINA: Men are always ready to throw themselves at the feet of an actress.

[*Dorn hums irritably.*]

Women have such a weakness for doctors.

DORN: Polina, some men—such as I—need the attention of women, not one woman, but women. I'm telling you this because I'm an honest man.

POLINA [*taking his hand*]: And a dear one, and I love you.

DORN: Thank you. The audience is assembling.

[*Enter, Arkadina on Sorin's arm, Trigorin, Shamrayev, Medvedenko, and Masha.*]

SHAMRAYEV: In 1873 at the Poltava fair she played astoundingly. Sheer delight.

ARKADINA: Who on earth do you mean?

SHAMRAYEV: Would you happen to know where Chadin—

ARKADINA: Who?

SHAMRAYEV: The comedian, Pavel Semyonovich Chadin, is at present? His Rasplyuev was inimitable, better than Sadovsky's I assure you, most esteemed lady. Where is he now?

ARKADINA: You keep asking me about these antediluvians. How should I know where he is? [*She sits.*]

SHAMRAYEV: The theatre has declined, Irina Nikolayevna! In the old days there were mighty oaks, but nowadays we see nothing but stumps.

ARKADINA: I find that remark somewhat offensive—

DORN: There are fewer brilliant talents today, that's true . . .

ARKADINA: I disagree with that. I don't know how you people in the country can pretend to be authorities on theatre.

SHAMRAYEV: It's a matter of taste, Madam. *De gustibus aut bene, aut nihil.* *

[*Constantine appears.*]

ARKADINA: My dear son, when is it going to begin? These men are deliberately insulting me. Please get on with it, Kostya.

CONSTANTINE: In a moment. Have a little patience, please.

---

*The pretentious Shamrayev, trying to show that he is as cultured as his employers, confuses two Latin proverbs: *De gustibus non est disputandum* ("About taste—it's no matter. for debate") and *De mortuis nihil nisi bonum* ("Of the dead [say] nothing but good"), and comes up with "About taste—either its good, or it's nothing."

ARKADINA: My son! [*reciting from* Hamlet]:
>"*Hamlet, speak no more!*
>*Thou turn'st mine eyes into my very soul;*
>*And there I see such black and grained spots*
>*As will not leave their tinct.*"

CONSTANTINE [*paraphrasing* Hamlet]:
>*Nay but to live*
>*In wickedness, to seek love*
>*In the depths of sin* . . .

[*A horn is sounded behind the stage.*]

Ladies and gentlemen, we are about to begin. Attention please! [*Pause.*] I shall begin. [*He taps a stick and recites.*] Oh, you ancient venerable shades, that float above the lake by night, darken our eyes with sleep, and bring us dreams of what will be two hundred thousand years from now.

SORIN [*sorrowfully*]: There'll be nothing two hundred thousand years from now or something worse than nothing. Of course, for each of us here assembled—Kostya, let me speak to you a moment.

CONSTANTINE: One moment! —What is it, Uncle? [*He draws Sorin aside.*]

SORIN [*whispering*]: I interrupted to warn you. Unless you invite her up on the stage, she's not going to like the performance.

CONSTANTINE: What would she do on the stage?

SORIN: Let her improvise something or, or—perform as a chorus, it will make all the difference in her response, you know.

Otherwise—you're such a sensitive boy and if she doesn't appreciate it, compares it unfavorably to that writer she goes about with, you'll be so depressed that—

ARKADINA [*rising and mounting the steps to the platform*]: Since there seems to be some delay—

CONSTANTINE: Mother, please stay off the stage!

[*She draws herself up regally.*]

ARKADINA: This makeshift platform a stage? It creaks underfoot. Why, that poor girl, she could have a serious injury up here in this dim light, and I would be sued to the hilt.

CONSTANTINE: Nina is young and she's light as a bird, which you're not, if you'll forgive me, Mother.

[*Trigorin rises and goes up to Arkadina on the stage.*]

TRIGORIN [*whispering to her, urgently*]: Be kind tonight, it's their night, you've had so many stages, allow them to have this platform, Irina.

ARKADINA: I merely wanted—

[*Trigorin virtually drags her down from the platform.*]

TRIGORIN: I know, I know, but—

ARKADINA: This happens to be my property, this is my estate.

SORIN: Not yet, sister, not yet. The estate is still mine for a while.

ARKADINA: Who pays the taxes on it?

[*The curtain rises on a view of the lake, moonlight, and Nina all in white.*]

NINA [*in a tremulous voice*]: Do I begin now or has it been called off?

CONSTANTINE: Begin!

NINA [*in a whisper*]: Man and lion . . .

CONSTANTINE: Speak a bit louder, don't be afraid— *Begin*!

NINA: Man and lion, eagle and quail, deer, geese, spiders, the silent fish dwelling in the deep, starfish and tiny creatures invisible to the eye, these and every form of life, every form of life; every form of life has ended its round of sorrow and become extinct.

ARKADINA [*in a loud whisper*]: So! A recitative!

[*Nina pauses.*]

CONSTANTINE: Continue.

NINA: Where was I?

CONSTANTINE [*prompting her*]: For thousands of—

NINA: Thousands of . . . ?

CONSTANTINE: For thousands of centuries . . .

NINA [*continuing rapidly, her voice trembling but with something that suggests her passion for theatre*]: For thousands of centuries the earth has borne no living creature. In vain now does this poor moon light her lamp. No longer do the cranes wake and cry in the meadow; and in the linden groves the hum of beetles is no longer heard. All is cold.

ARKADINA: Decadence!

TRIGORIN: Shhh.

SHAMRAYEV: She's right about that.

NINA: And empty, terrible. [*She sneezes three times.*]

[*Pause.*]

The bodies of all living beings have dissolved into dust. Eternal matter has transformed them into stone, water, and cloud, and their spirits are merged into one.

SHAMRAYEV: How uncomfortable.

NINA: I, I am the soul of the world. In me is the spirit of Alexander the Great, of Caesar, of Shakespeare, Napoleon, and of the lowest form of worm.

DORN: Well, that's an abrupt descent for us.

NINA: In me, the consciousness of man and the instincts of the animals are one. I remember everything, everything. In me, each life lives . . .

[*Arkadina springs up and approaches her son.*]

ARKADINA: Kostya, let me speak to her, the girl is in a panic!

CONSTANTINE [*in an imploring whisper*]: Go back and stay in your seat.

ARKADINA [*with a dramatic shrug, returning*]: The boy is impudent, and I'm sorry but the work is worthless.

NINA: I am alone.

CONSTANTINE: You've skipped a page.

DORN: Fortunately.

NINA: Once in a hundred years I open my mouth to speak. My voice echoes dolefully in this void and no one hears it. Until then horror, horror. Behold my powerful enemy Satan approaches. I see his terrible blood-red eyes. [*One worker holds up two red lanterns, while another mixes bottles for "smoke."*]

ARKADINA: Sulfur, a smell of sulfur, I'm strangling, I can't endure it, my throat—

CONSTANTINE [*wildly*]: *Enough, enough*! Nina, my mother has—

ARKADINA: My throat is indispensable to my profession—its a delicate organ.

[*Constantine mounts the stage: the curtain is jerked down.*]

TRIGORIN: Irina, the throat is not an organ.

ARKADINA: Mine has often been compared to an organ!—in its richness and range! You know that.

[*Constantine leaps off the stage to confront his mother.*]

CONSTANTINE: Do please forgive me, both of you, for my presumption tonight. I'd overlooked the fact that art is a monopoly, exclusively for the few that God's ordained to act or to write—and I'm not one, I could never be one! Forgive my audacity! [*He staggers as if drunk upstage to the bench.*]

ARKADINA [*innocently*]: Now what provoked this outburst?

SORIN: Irina, my dear, you shouldn't wound a young man's pride like that.

ARKADINA: Don't call it pride, it is vanity, *vanitas vanitatum*! Boris, Boris, where are you going?

[*Boris goes up to Constantine.*]

TRIGORIN: Kostya, Kostya, may I speak to you?

CONSTANTINE: No, no, stay with my mother, console her! She's in distress. [*Constantine stares fiercely at Trigorin for a moment and then rushes off alone.*]

ARKADINA [*approaching*]: And so my son is demented!

TRIGORIN: Do you wish to destroy him?

ARKADINA: He *told* us that it was a joke.

SORIN: Out of modesty, out of fear of exactly the contemptuous attitude that you—

ARKADINA: Nonsense! You want me to bestow false praise on this nonsense? No, truth always. Truth is the only possible help to those aspiring to what is out of their reach and—

TRIGORIN: Since when could you take truth?

ARKADINA [*stunned*]: Since—what?

[*Nina comes in shyly.*]

SORIN: Bravo, bravo!

ARKADINA: Yes, bravo. You did the best you could without any training, my dear, you must not feel humiliated. After all, a recitative is the most demanding thing that a trained actress undertakes. Why, even I, after all my professional experience on the stage, approach the recitative with trepidation. I have to draw on all of my resources to—

TRIGORIN: May I be introduced to the young star of the evening, Irina?

ARKADINA: Do excuse me! Nina Mikhailovna, may I present Boris Alekseyevich Trigorin.

NINA [*overcome with embarrassment*]: Oh, I'm so happy to—I'm always reading your— [*She stops, confused.*]

ARKADINA: Finish your sentences, dear.

NINA: I should think a person, people, with creative gifts, with—talents like yours would be terribly bored with—

ARKADINA: Now, my dear, don't embarrass him, Boris can't bear such effusions.

SORIN: Could they raise that curtain? —It looks so sinister now.

NINA: I'm afraid it must have seemed a very strange play.

TRIGORIN: Yes, being in a new form but fascinating, and beautifully—recited.

ARKADINA: Nina, you came here in a carriage I presume?

NINA: No, I walked, I love walking and anyway our carriage—

ARKADINA: I understand. Your father's new wife had undoubtedly gone for a drive. Well, you must go home in ours, you must be exhausted. We won't delay you.

NINA: I must say something to Kostya, something, I, but, I don't know what.

ARKADINA: Reserve it for an evening when he's less hysterical and you're not so out of breath, and when I see you again, do remind me to give you some exercises in breathing.

NINA: —Goodnight, Sir.

TRIGORIN: You live near here?

NINA: You can see my father's house, just beyond the birch grove that we call Silver Point!

SORIN: Sister? You'll say a few words to your son?

ARKADINA: Yes, but they will be honest. There's nothing more tragic than the pursuit of a profession for which you've no apparent talent.

SORIN: That's not true of—

ARKADINA: Petrusha, how would you know? I've known young men and women who devoted their lives to hopes of becoming artists. Discovered they lacked the talent too late to find occupations of a kind to which they were suited by nature. Isn't that so, Boris?—Boris! I'm speaking to you!

TRIGORIN: Nina was pointing her home out to me. It's a large house and white as bone in the moonlight.

ARKADINA: A mausoleum is what it—never, never look at it, *ça porte malheur*! Forgive me, Nina. I can't help recalling the suffering of your mother.

NINA: I'm afraid she wanted to go long before she was taken.

ARKADINA: I know, I know, don't remind me. Child, if you don't go straight to our carriage, that tyrant Shamrayev will send it back to the stables.

NINA [*to Trigorin*]: Goodnight. [*She exits.*]

SHAMRAYEV: I recall one evening at the opera house in Moscow when the famous Silva took a low C. It so happened that the bass from our church choir was sitting in the gallery, and suddenly—you can imagine our utter amazement—we heard: "Bravo, Silva" from the gallery—but a whole octave lower! Like this [*in a deep bass*]: "Bravo, Silva" . . . The audience was thunderstruck. [*Pause.*]

DORN: The angel of silence has flown over us.

ARKADINA: That girl is doomed. Some people are so thoroughly doomed that it's a contagion, it's dangerous to stay near them. Her mother left her entire, enormous fortune, yes, every last kopeck, to her father, a man who brought his mistresses into the house before his wife died; married a girl half his age, no better than a harlot, he's left her all in his will, his daughter nothing.

TRIGORIN: Excuse me, I'll see her to the carriage and then say a few words to Kostya.

SORIN [*rubbing his hands to warm them*]: Let's go, let's go. It's so damp. My legs ache.

ARKADINA: Well, come along you poor old man. [*She takes his arm.*] You must remember that I'm tired. And I'm temperamental even with my son. You know how much I love him.

SHAMRAYEV [*offering his arm to his wife*]: Madam?

SORIN: I hear that dog howling again. [*To Shamrayev*]: Ilya Afanasyevich, be so good as to let it off the chain.

SHAMRAYEV: Can't be done, Pyotr Nikolayevich, I'm afraid of thieves breaking into the barn. I've got millet in there. [*To Medvedenko, walking beside him*]: Yes, a whole octave lower: "Bravo Silva!" And not even a singer mind you, just an ordinary church chorister.

MEDVEDENKO: Church chorister? How much do they get paid?

[*All go out except Dorn. Enter Constantine.*]

CONSTANTINE: *Nina*!!

DORN: Whew, what a nervous boy you are, tears in your eyes!

CONSTANTINE: Have you never been hurt by the mockery of—

DORN [*cutting in*]: Madame Arkadina?

CONSTANTINE: My mother.

DORN: But tears, tears! They're for women.

CONSTANTINE: All human beings can be injured and outraged to the point of tears, Doctor Dorn. Of course that may not apply to you.

DORN: You can't make interesting theatre out of abstract ideas. And stage effects that include sulfur. It's laughable, excuse me, but—

CONSTANTINE: Where's Nina?

DORN: Gone, I should think. It was hardly a night of glory for your actress, either. [*He leaves, chuckling, towards the house.*]

CONSTANTINE [*calling out hoarsely*]: Nina? Nina?

[*Trigorin appears upstage and approaches Constantine.*]

TRIGORIN: Ah, there you are, Constantine.

[*Constantine starts to move away.*]

We've all extended our congratulations to the young lady.

CONSTANTINE: Where is she?

TRIGORIN: I've put her in a carriage.

CONSTANTINE: She didn't wait to see me.

TRIGORIN: She wanted to, but I'm afraid your mother was determined to get her home quickly.

CONSTANTINE: Perhaps it's just as well. There wasn't much to be said.

TRIGORIN: About your writing, and writing in general, may I speak to you a little?

CONSTANTINE: Why?

TRIGORIN: I understand your present mood but—I do want you to know that I was moved by the intensity of feeling in the piece. Do you realize how young you are? You have a lot of time to learn the discipline of writing as a craft. You already have the talent, you must simply go on, go on, regardless of frivolous reactions.

[*Masha appears upstage.*]

MASHA: Constantine, your mother wants to speak to you, she's afraid you misunderstood her.

CONSTANTINE: Tell her I've gone away, and please, all of you, leave me alone, don't keep coming after me with these bits of consolation, scraps thrown to a whipped dog. [*He exits. Masha starts to follow, calling:*]

MASHA: Constantine, Kostya . . . [*Masha bursts into tears.*]

TRIGORIN: And so you care for him too.

[*Pause. Music.*]

MASHA: Care for him? I love Constantine much more than my own life . . .

TRIGORIN: Youth, youth!

MASHA: When there's nothing else to say, people always say "youth, youth."

TRIGORIN: How tortured you both are by it. And by love. Unrequited . . . Well. Youth, love, they're worth the price, worth it no matter what a . . . How bewitching the lake is! It's telling you something. What the lake tells us is what God tells us—we just don't know his language.

DIM OUT

The scene takes place in the garden, which is set with summer lawn furniture. It is midday. The remains of a picnic are suggested: picnic basket, cloth. Dorn is reading to Arkadina and Masha.

DORN [*reading*]: ". . . for society people to pamper novelists and entice them into their own circle is as dangerous as for corn merchants to breed rats in their barns."

ARKADINA [*to Masha*]: Come, let's stand up. Side by side. You're twenty-one and I am nearly twice that. Doctor Dorn, which of us looks older?

DORN [*winking at Masha*]: What age did you say you are, Madam Arkadina?

ARKADINA [*angrily*]: I am going to stop serving wine at lunch! It makes you all dull and witless. I did not mention my age.

DORN: You shouldn't be so sensitive about it.

ARKADINA: Are you deliberately not understanding what I—?

DORN: Not at all, my dear lady— You're flushed, sit down— Now it's only here at the country place that it's known you have a son twenty-five years of age. It's not even known in town. Why, yesterday the chemist's wife said to me, "I can't believe that Madam Arkadina's over fifty!" —What are you laughing at, Masha?

MASHA: You're inclined to be cruel at times.

ARKADINA: No more wine at lunch. And I shall keep the key to the liquor cabinet in my strongbox.

[*Masha is laughing behind her hand.*]

You may be amused. I am not— I am not vain about my youthful appearance. It's attributable to work! Keeping on the go, the *qui vive*! Make it a rule not to contemplate the future, no, ignore the future as if it didn't exist. Such things as old age and death? Oh, who is immortal!

DORN: Possibly you, dear lady. Having cheated the years so successfully up till now, why shouldn't it be conceivable that your luck will hold with what's regarded as the final fate.

MASHA [*in a half whisper*]: I haven't the slightest desire to go on.

DORN [*who is flirting with Masha*]: You're indulging in melancholia. I have a prescription for that. [*He leans towards her.*] —Drop by my office before it opens tomorrow or after it closes.

MASHA: You wish me to replace my mother in your alleged affections? —Ha, no! You're not the dashing young Casanova you take yourself for.

ARKADINA: What's going on here?

DORN: Nothing of consequence, Madam.

[*Arkadina has risen and is pacing about like a peacock.*]

ARKADINA: I keep myself in hand. Always dressed correctly for the occasion. My hair, abundant, not a single hair faded.

DORN: The chemist's wife's younger than you, dear lady, but she's almost gray.

ARKADINA: —What?

DORN: Nothing— Masha?

ARKADINA: Would I step out of the house, even here in the garden, in a negligee, without dressing my hair? Never! — When a woman is dowdy, she's let go of her life. Watch how I walk! [*She continues strutting, arms akimbo.*] —Light as a bird, could play a girl of fifteen.

DORN [*aside to Masha*]: Her problem's self-delusion, yours melancholia. Yours I can treat successfully if—

ARKADINA: What *are* you two whispering about?

DORN: Just wondered where the book is.

MASHA [*coldly*]: In your hand.

DORN: Ah, well, now, where'd we leave off? Ohhh, yessss— Corn merchants and rats! —How exciting a subject!

ARKADINA: Give me the book, I'll read, your voice is slurred. And the rats . . . Here it is . . . [*She reads.*] "And it goes without saying that for society people to pamper novelists and entice them into their own circle is as dangerous as for corn merchants to breed rats in their barns. And yet they are loved. Thus, when a woman has chosen a writer whom she wishes to capture, she lays siege to him by means of compliments, courtesies, and favors . . ." Well, that may be true of the French, but we're not that calculating. Here a woman is usually in love with a writer before she sets out to capture him. To go no further, take Trigorin and me . . .

[*Enter Sorin, leaning on a cane, with Nina at his side. Medvedenko pushes an empty wheelchair after them.*]

SORIN [*in the caressing tone one uses to a child*]: Yes? We're delighted, aren't we? And we're cheerful today, and all that sort of thing? [*To his sister*]: We're delighted! Nina's father and stepmother have gone off to Tver, and now we're free for three whole days. Isn't that so, Nina?

[*Nina sits down beside Arkadina and embraces her.*]

NINA: Yes and I'm so happy! Now I belong to you. I belong to this house.

DORN: She's looking very pretty today, isn't she Madam?

ARKADINA: And very smartly dressed, interesting . . . There's a clever girl. [*She kisses her.*] But we mustn't praise her too much—it's bad luck, you know. Where is Boris Alekseyevich?

NINA: He's down by the lake, fishing.

ARKADINA: Wouldn't you think he'd be bored with fish? Tell me, what is the matter with my son? Why is he so moody? He spends whole days by the lake. I hardly ever see him.

MASHA: He's an emotional man. [*To Nina, timidly*]: Nina, please read something from his play again.

NINA [*shrugging her shoulders*]: Do you really want me to? After the other time?

MASHA [*restraining her enthusiasm*]: When he reads anything himself, his eyes shine with feeling. He has a beautiful, sad voice and the manner of a poet. He is a poet.

[*Sorin can be heard snoring.*]

DORN: The pronouncement is made. Good night.

ARKADINA: Petrusha!

SORIN: Eh?

ARKADINA: Are you asleep?

SORIN: Not at all.

[*Pause.*]

ARKADINA: Perhaps you'd help Petrusha. He's getting no sort of medical treatment and each time I come back here I notice he's more depressed and less active. It breaks my heart!

SORIN: I'd gladly try any treatment but your devoted friend, Yevgeny, advises me to reconcile myself to my illnesses, whatever they are.

DORN: I'm sorry, but your condition isn't a thing that medicine can improve. Oh, charlatans, they'd give you sugar pills, but a reputable physician doesn't practice deception on a man of your age.

SORIN: My age is only sixty and I wish to live on.

ARKADINA: How about mineral baths? There's a mineral spring not far from here. Wouldn't that do some good?

DORN: It might and it might not.

MEDVEDENKO: At least he should give up smoking.

DORN: I tell you it makes no difference if he does or doesn't. I'm sorry to say that I can recommend nothing at all to help him.

SORIN: All you prescribe for me is—resignation. Prescription rejected! You're resigned to nothing. Live a dissolute life of—self-indulgence. Oh, sometime you'll pay the fiddler. But you'll dance merrily on, philosophical stuff like—resignation! surrender!—to a man who'd had not one single thing in his life, not even in his youth!—to give him any feeling of having accomplished anything he hoped for!

ARKADINA: Petrusha, don't complain so bitterly, so loudly.

SORIN: Why not? Who cares but me? Would it please you all if I waded out in the lake and just—floated away? I—I sometimes get that impression.

ARKADINA: Petrusha, come sit by me. You know how precious you are to us all.

SORIN: Oh, yes, I know, I know . . . All of you so healthy, with achievements to look back on and more to come but I—not even the remembrance of much pleasure when I was young. No, not even then . . .

ARKADINA: Petrusha, you've had a devoted sister who's known here and abroad. But still is happiest near you. Dear friends, it's so good to be near you for a while—so warm, so quiet, evenings of nothing but lotto and philosophy, rounded off by completely

undisturbed sleep. Wonderful for a while but for a while only—
Then cities and theatre again, I must confess how vitalizing it is
to have that to go back to! —My career! —My life!

NINA: Yes, yes! —I understand you so well! If only—

[*Enter Shamrayev, followed by his wife, Polina.*]

SHAMRAYEV: Greetings, greetings! [*He turns to Arkadina.*]
My wife tells me you want to drive in town but I regret to tell
you that we're carting rye today, all men, all horses, indispensable to me.

ARKADINA: But I have, as I told you, an appointment with the
woman who treats my hair. And I intend to keep it.

SHAMRAYEV: My dear lady, you refuse to understand what
farming means.

ARKADINA: This is entirely too much, this is insulting. I, I—I
shall leave at once for Moscow! Will you order me horses from
the village or must I walk to the station?

SHAMRAYEV: Impossible! —I resign! You and your brother must
look for another steward. [*He stalks back toward the house.*]

SORIN: I tell you that man's insolence is beyond everything.

[*Arkadina rushes to the house.*]

ARKADINA: Boris! Boris we're leaving.

SORIN: Have all the horses brought here at once! [*He stamps
his cane. Polina bursts into tears.*]

POLINA: I'm helpless, helpless! Put yourself in my position! What can I do with that man?

NINA: How does he dare to address Irina Nikolayevna in such a manner?

[*Sorin attempts to rise.*]

Uncle, you're shaking! We'll wheel your chair back to the house! I tell you, it's almost as dreadful, as shocking, as the situation I live in at home . . .

SORIN: Oh, yes, it's dreadful—but he can't leave anymore than I can escape.

[*They go off. Dorn and Polina are left alone.*]

POLINA: Yevgeny? Our time is passing. Once you wanted me to come and live with you, but Masha was so young then. Now I could—for what's left of our lives.

DORN: Oh Lord, tears. Don't show them here to be noticed and talked of.

POLINA: How is it possible that a woman can find a man despicable as I find you, *know* you to be, and yet—still long to be with him? For both of us time is passing, yes for you, too, despite your cologne and talcum, your suave social manner. Why, I've heard you go to a barber daily to help you keep up this illusion of youth. Still—illusion's not truth.

DORN: I am fifty.

POLINA: *Five.* Are you planning a stage career? Is that why you try to pass yourself off for younger than—

DORN: If I look at the most fifty, then I am at the most fifty and if you look your age, it's your punishment for taking the joke of human existence as a serious matter. Now here comes true youth!

[*Nina appears upstage with a bouquet of wild flowers.*]

POLINA: I'd advise you not to try your charms on her.

DORN: Young lady patients are often as susceptible as those older—and more attractive. [*He rises and crosses toward Nina.*] Well, how are things going in there, I hope that calm is restored, I don't like emotional outbursts.

NINA: Irina Nikolayevna is crying and Pyotr Nikolayevich is having an attack of asthma.

DORN: While you have the good sense to gather an armful of flowers.

NINA: For you if you—

DORN: *Merci bien.*

[*Polina has crossed to him.*]

DORN: Now if you'll excuse me for just a moment or two I'll administer some drops of valerian to the great actress and her brother.

POLINA: Give me the flowers, I will find a vase for them. [*She snatches them from Dorn and strides quickly off, tearing them savagely to pieces, and flinging them away. Nina stands looking out, bemused, at the lake. Dorn adjusts his hair or cravat and descends the steps to her.*]

NINA: Back so quickly? Doctor, I don't understand how a famous actress could cry for such a trivial reason.

DORN: Oh, women's tears—mean nothing.

NINA: And that such a celebrated author such as Boris Trigorin should spend the whole day fishing and be delighted that he has caught two chub? I thought that such people as he and Irina were of a totally different world.

DORN [*impatiently*]: Oh, they are, they are. My dear, you're looking a bit pale—

NINA [*ignoring him*]: But here they are, crying, fishing, playing cards, laughing, and losing their tempers.

DORN: You need a tonic, my dear. I'm heavily booked today but if you could drop by my office, say, at half past six— Oh Lord, here comes the desperate young poet— I shall expect you?

[*Constantine stops short, glaring at Dorn.*]

Ah, my dear Constantine. When will you favor us with a new entertainment?

CONSTANTINE: Will you be so good as to return to the house or to—wherever you're going?

DORN: Temperament! —Invariable sign of genius. [*He exits, crossly.*]

CONSTANTINE: Christ! —Playing up to you, was he? Notorious old lecher! If I had another shot left in this gun— [*Pause. He abruptly drops the dead bird at her feet. She utters a startled cry.*]

NINA: What's this? What does this mean?

[*He picks up the bird and holds it towards her. She stares at him, speechless.*]

CONSTANTINE: Well? See what I've done? Shot this sea gull!

NINA: By accident?

CONSTANTINE: No.

NINA: Then I don't understand. Oh, don't hold it out to me, what's the matter with you? You look so wild I—hardly recognize you.

CONSTANTINE: I find you equally changed—you treat me with absolute indifference, my presence seems to embarrass you.

NINA: You know you're not acting normally, Kostya. You, you—are you talking in symbols, and is presenting me with this dead bird one of them? Well, I'm afraid I'm too simple a person to interpret the symbol.

CONSTANTINE: This all began, this, this—alienation between us—the evening my play was laughed at. You left without a word to me and you've avoided me since then— Women never forgive a failure.

NINA: I'm not a woman, I'm—just a confused girl, Kostya.

CONSTANTINE: The play, I tore it to bits.

NINA: I don't think I can listen to any more of this, Kostya. [*She starts away: he restrains her.*]

CONSTANTINE: Don't you care what you've done to me, don't you know or care? I can't believe it!—it's as if you'd fallen under somebody's spell. [*He glances off.*] And I think I see your spell-binder approaching. I won't stand in your way. [*He exits. Trigorin enters with his notebook.*]

TRIGORIN: Good afternoon, Miss Nina. I hope I didn't drive your young friend away.

NINA: Good afternoon, sir. No. He—I can't make any sense of his talk or behavior lately.

TRIGORIN: Still upset over the play?

NINA: I honestly don't know. Let's not discuss it right now.

[*Arkadina is heard calling out, "Where's Boris?"*]

TRIGORIN: Irina suddenly wants to leave the lake and I'd just got hold of a story, characters half substantial and half shadow but—sorry, you're not a writer.

NINA: Unfortunately, I have no creative—accomplishment, oh, a great longing to be an actress, but—must you leave here today?

TRIGORIN: Yes, we're off again on the long, tedious trail to her next engagement.

NINA: Perhaps—perhaps you can use the time on the train to complete your story.

TRIGORIN [*after a desperate pause*]: *Ha ha ha ah ah!* Use the time? On the train? In our lady's compartment while she studies her part? The part of Medea? Howls? Lamentations? "Please, dear, not quite so loud." —"Shall I try to find a different compartment?" "Boris, Boris, just hear this! Then go!" —I am subjected to a tirade. "No, no, overdid, did I?" —"Yes, dear, just slightly." —"Suppose I begin on a lower key?" — "Yes, on a much lower key and continue on that key and try to end on that key." —The train has stopped, I'm getting off for coffee. "Boris, don't be so rude, don't presume too far on familiar association. When you are traveling with a lady, is it not proper to inquire, 'May I get you some coffee?'" —Excuse this—outburst, I'm not ready to go.

NINA: —Then—stay. Can't she go on ahead?

TRIGORIN: Young lady? Of the lake? —I'm afraid the situation is far more complicated than you could imagine or I could explain if—I dared to—

NINA: My, uh, surroundings, yes, this lake and my father's house—our few little—distractions, card games, theatrical improvisations, sometimes a written scene. But—

TRIGORIN: —Yes?

NINA: There is the—interior—world . . .

41

TRIGORIN: —Be careful of it. It can be invaded and haunted . . .

NINA: It's clear to me that you're not—at all ready to— leave . . .

TRIGORIN: If it were likely that we would meet again and for more time the next time—Oh, I feel, I suddenly felt when you said "interior world" that we could—talk of—more than I had imagined . . .

NINA: —You won't come back?

TRIGORIN: Only if there is a suitable interval in her professional schedule—but she's a popular star and as she gets a bit older and thinks more about staying young—well—theatre is increasingly her obsession.

NINA: As yours is writing.

TRIGORIN: Exactly.

NINA: Two corresponding obsessions—two people devoted to art—

TRIGORIN: And in her heart and my heart, a secret distrust of—

NINA: —What?

TRIGORIN: The true worth of what we're doing. Oh. Shut me up. I get overwrought sometimes . . .

NINA: Why not take a vacation by yourself?

TRIGORIN: Should I do that—and I've tried, a telegram would come to me—"Please, please, please, come back—going to pieces" . . . I've had a week off the leash. Even possibly two. But back I come, fearing she's suffered some grievous misfortune—of the kind, nothing. Bursting with satisfaction, a triumph unprecedented in all her career—according to her.

NINA: Are you telling me you're not altogether happy with this—arrangement?

TRIGORIN: —You express yourself maturely for such a young girl—I don't often meet young girls with grown-up intuitions. I've forgotten how it feels to be eighteen or nineteen. I can't picture it very clearly, that's why the young girls in my novels and stories are generally false. I've forgotten my youth at the age of thirty-seven.

NINA: You look so much younger. Almost as young as—Kostya . . .

TRIGORIN: Take care of each other. He's as vulnerable as you—possibly even more—

NINA: He has a feeling for me I can't return.

TRIGORIN: Which is—

NINA: Something more than—

TRIGORIN: Affection?

NINA: Yes, I feel deep affection, sometimes I feel a fear for him but—love, no . . .

TRIGORIN: —Perhaps after this meeting I'll be able to write more knowingly about girls, perhaps I can bring them to life.

NINA: Oh, no, I—you're so mistaken. May I say you're the only writer of my acquaintance who understands the female character.

TRIGORIN: You're a beautiful and very kind young girl. I took part in a rather, actually a very—interesting discussion at a cafe in Moscow that's popular with writers and other artists. Somebody said there are some writers who can't create convincing female characters and, Boris you're one of the few who can. [*He laughs sadly.*] I felt myself flushing—embarrassed. You see, I knew that he didn't like me and always disparaged my work. He went on to say that I had a certain softness about me, in my eyes and—Well. He was implying that I was deficient in— virility for—the practice of such a totally masculine profession as that of writing. I realized that. I stopped blushing. I looked at him, straight in the eyes and I doubt that my eyes were soft then. I said to him, "You are excessively delicate in your attack on me for a change. Now why is that? What do you really mean? I doubt that I don't know or anyone at this table doesn't know, so why hesitate to say it straight out like the shameless hack you are?"
He said nothing. I went on staring straight at him. Finally he did speak— A single obscene word, drank down his wine and spat it onto my face . . .
If I said to you that I think that a writer needs a bit of both sexes in him? —No. —You're not a writer. —About writing, it's not an enviable—obsession because it is just that, an obsession— You live from one work to the next, haunted always by—am I finished? Will there be another?
And you are someone in the hands of others who ask themselves the same question that you ask yourself but in such a dif-

ferent way. You ask yourself the question because without a new work to turn to, your life would be absent completely. But they ask the question because if you did not produce the new work, you'd no longer be of financial value or any interest to them.

A writer's a madman, probationally released— And yet when I'm writing, I do enjoy it. Even reading the proofs, but—when I see it in print, I'm—devastated. It falls so far short of the mark I'd set for myself, I—I'm so profoundly depressed, I must run to, to—Sicily or to Venice or a Greek island and—turn for a while into a simply—mindless—beast . . .

—You know, when I die people that walk by my grave will say, "Here lies Trigorin, a good writer in his way but a far cry from Tolstoy or Turgenev." —And I'd agree.

NINA: —Can't it be you're simply spoiled by success, a writer translated in foreign languages, admired by thousands, by—thousands . . .

TRIGORIN: I would prefer, much prefer, to be loved by—

NINA: —By?

TRIGORIN [*touching her face*]: One . . .

NINA: You mean as a—

TRIGORIN: Known and completely understood by just one.

NINA: You're not able to see that you are?

[*Pause.*]

TRIGORIN: What's this?

NINA: A dead sea gull.

45

TRIGORIN: There's blood on it. Was it—?

NINA: I don't know why, but Constantine shot it and he— presented it to me . . .

[*Trigorin bends to pick the dead bird up gently.*]

TRIGORIN: I don't know which to feel sorrier for, Kostya, or— this beautiful dead bird— Why'd he present it to you? I understand things that happen in Moscow cafes, but this is a—mystery to me. A mystery that intrigues me. I don't want to leave here.

NINA: Then don't!

[*Arkadina is heard shouting for him.*]

TRIGORIN: Who could defy a summons such as that? [*He takes out his notebook and scribbles something in it.*]

NINA: What are you writing?

TRIGORIN: Just making a note of an idea for a story which occurred to me. A lovely young girl—lives all her life, by a lake— that's enchanting. She loves it as a sea gull and like a sea gull, she's happy and free. But—a man comes along by chance and, having nothing better to do, he—

ARKADINA [*offstage, shouting from the house*]: Boris, Boris, where *are* you?

TRIGORIN: *Coming*! [*He starts upstage.*] *What is it?*

ARKADINA [*offstage*]: We're staying— Did you hear me?

[*Trigorin returns to Nina.*]

TRIGORIN: Did anyone ever fail to hear the lady? They can catch every syllable of that voice in the second gallery.

[*There is a slight pause.*]

NINA: —You were saying that a man comes along by chance and—

TRIGORIN: Destroys her— Watch out, it could happen.

ARKADINA [*offstage*]: *Boris!*

TRIGORIN: *Coming!* [*The sound of a loon is heard.*] How lovely it is. How bewitching. [*Piano music begins.*] Especially with the mist rising . . . A loon cries out, there is stirring in the leaves and someone is playing a *valse triste* on the piano. Who is it?

NINA: Kostya.

TRIGORIN: Your companion of the lake . . .

NINA: The lake must let me go and so must Kostya. Of course they're as you describe them, romantically misty—

TRIGORIN: Mysterious as dreams—

NINA: But I have to escape them if I'm ever to accomplish my life . . . Surely you understand. What don't you understand?

TRIGORIN: I do understand your wanting to leave some day. But I hope that when you leave for the excitement, the lights of what is called the world—cities, theatres, cafes—I hope most earnestly it won't turn bitter and you won't be haunted as I am—by the regrets and—the guilt of abandoning someone or something—that held you in a dream. Forgive me these sentiments, Nina—it's only the music, the mist . . .

ARKADINA [*offstage, calling imperiously*]: Boris!

TRIGORIN: Yes, set up the table for lotto!

ARKADINA [*offstage*]: We're not yet leaving. Can you hear me?

TRIGORIN: You told me.

ARKADINA [*offstage*]: We're staying a while longer. I've just been informed that the theatre's not been redecorated as I insisted and they haven't even begun work on my costumes! It's absolutely . . .

[*During this Trigorin, chuckling, starts toward the house, pausing to look back at Nina, and exits.*]

NINA: A dream.

DIM OUT

ACT THREE

The dining room in Sorin's house: doors are indicated on the right and left. A sideboard is visible, and a table is in the middle of the room. On the floor are a trunk and hat boxes—signs of preparation for departure. Trigorin is having lunch; Masha is standing by the table. Servants are taking luggage to the carriage.

MASHA: I'm telling all of you this.

TRIGORIN: There's only myself and you.

MASHA: —Good. You're a writer and maybe you can use it. If Kostya had wounded himself fatally, I wouldn't have gone on living another minute.

TRIGORIN: You have more courage than that.

MASHA: But he's not as seriously hurt as I've been for a long time. And now I've made up my mind to tear this impossible love out of my heart by the roots.

TRIGORIN: How are you going to do that?

MASHA [*pouring herself another vodka*]: I'm going to get married.

TRIGORIN: Oh? To whom?

MASHA: The school master—Medvedenko.

TRIGORIN: Are you reconciled to an action as drastic as that?

MASHA: You've never loved without hope?

TRIGORIN: Never with much.

MASHA: Spent whole years waiting to be given more than—casual—attention. Marriage will at least give me new concerns that will partially distract me from the old ones. A change, at least a change— Shall we have another?

TRIGORIN: You haven't had enough, Masha?

MASHA: To live with this sudden decision? Marriage to a school master who thinks that Hamlet's an English actor, talks constantly of being underpaid?

TRIGORIN: Sit down. Give me that carafe.

MASHA [*retreating from him*]: Don't you know women drink more than suspected? Not as openly as I do—most of them in secret. Always vodka or cognac. Why? Why? A compromise like giving myself to Medvedenko, sharing his house, his—bed! And wish me luck! Listening, listening to him! A life sentence of it!

TRIGORIN: There's a way to pretend to. Just say, "Yes? Yes? Yes?" —Without really hearing a word. I know, I've done it. Become an old hand at it.

MASHA: Good luck! —You're wonderful to talk to. You listen. Boris Alekseyevich? —What's your impression of me, how do I—look to you?

TRIGORIN: Much superior to the—bargain you say you've made. But—I hope it will be endurable to you. A thing that's endurable is not so easy to come by . . .

MASHA: Can't you persuade your—?

TRIGORIN: —No. She won't stay now. Her son is behaving most strangely. First he shoots himself, and now they say he's going to challenge me to a duel. And for what? Because I'm a writer? But there's room for all, the old and new.

MASHA: Well, there's jealousy. However, that's not my affair.

[*Pause. Yakov crosses from right to left carrying a suitcase.*]

My school master is none too clever, but he's kind, and a poor soul, and he loves me very much. I'm sorry for him. And I'm sorry for his old mother. Well, I wish you all the best. Don't think badly of me.

[*Nina enters.*]

I'm very grateful to you for spending this time with me. Would it be too much to ask you to send me one of your books—and write this in it. "To Maria, who doesn't know where she comes from and why she is living in this world." [*She sees Nina approaching.*] Good-bye. [*She exits.*]

NINA [*extending the fist of one hand*]: Odd or even.

TRIGORIN: Even.

NINA [*laughing*]: I was trying to tell whether to go on the stage or not.

TRIGORIN: That's something you can't decide by the number of peas in your hand.

NINA: Can't you advise me about it? After all you've seen of theatre—life?

TRIGORIN: —I don't dare give advice on such a serious subject. It's too momentous. Consequences, passions too dangerous. It's really a matter of how intensely you want to. Tell me. Why do you think Constantine shot himself? Masha said jealousy was involved in it. But jealousy of what?

NINA: I think some day you may guess. Meanwhile—and since you're leaving the lake again and I'm staying and one never knows if you'll come back—keep this little medallion as a remembrance of me? It has the title of a book of yours on the other side, *Nights and Days*.

TRIGORIN: A charming gift. [*He kisses the medallion.*] So Constantine *is* jealous, but why of me? Why aren't you attracted to such a romantically handsome young man who was driven to shoot himself for you?

NINA: We've grown up together. I'm too used to him as just a friend.

TRIGORIN: And you look at me, a man approaching middle age—

NINA: Without a sign of it. I'd hoped that you'd—someone's coming! Just in time to stop me from making an indiscreet confession.

TRIGORIN: Later?

NINA: Let me have just a minute or two alone with you before you leave, if you possibly can.

[*Enter Arkadina, Sorin, and Yakov busy with luggage.*]

ARKADINA: Petrusha, stay home, you're limping with rheumatism. [*To Trigorin*]: Who was it that just went out, was it Nina?

TRIGORIN [*casually*]: Yes, she was saying good-bye.

ARKADINA: Pardon our intrusion. Packed everything. [*The servants exchange looks.*] Exhausted . . .

YAKOV [*clearing the table*]: Am I to pack your fishing rods too?

TRIGORIN: Yes, I hope I'll be wanting them again.

YAKOV: Yes, sir.

TRIGORIN: Are there any copies of my books in the house?

ARKADINA: Yes, in the corner bookcase of my brother's study. Why?

TRIGORIN: Just wondered. [*To himself, reading the inscription on the medallion*]: Page one twenty-one— [*He exits.*]

SORIN: Not to Moscow, just to town.

ARKADINA: What's there going on in town?

SORIN: Laying of the cornerstone for the town hall.

ARKADINA: Just wet cement.

SORIN: I've been lying about like an old cigarette holder too long. As for Kostya, you know that you could take him to Moscow with you.

ARKADINA: Impossible, he's half out of his senses. Stay here, dear old man, take care of yourself and my son—I'm not leaving for good. Keep a watch on my son till he's in a calmer state. I'll never know why he tried to—made the silly, romantic young gesture of—

SORIN: Trying to kill himself.

ARKADINA: I suspect that jealousy was the first reason, that silly girl he's mad for, and—can you imagine!—she's after Boris Alekseyevich. The sooner I get Boris away from here the better.

SORIN: Sister, be a little more understanding. A young man of such intelligence, stuck here in this remote country place. Talented but with no chance to—no money to—he feels a parasite, a hanger-on. And has pride.

ARKADINA: —Why doesn't he go into military service, like most young men with—talent? —No, I don't see it . . .

SORIN: Just be so good as to give him a little money, enough to dress like a young gentleman which he is, not like a serf which he isn't! —And you could even afford to send him abroad to know a bit of the world away from this lake—be generous, sister, before it's—it could be too late . . .

ARKADINA: A suit of clothes, I might be able to manage that for him, but as for going abroad, he'd just get into trouble. Here, he's secure. Besides—you know how my money goes, the expenses of keeping up an appearance that is expected of me. [*She is at a glazed mirror, carefully pinning on an elaborate hat.*] I'm not sure I could even manage to buy him new clothes right now. That's how hard up I am.

[*Sorin laughs sadly.*]

What's so amusing?

SORIN: How much did you pay for that big ostrich-plumed hat?

ARKADINA: Don't you know that an actress in my position must wear Paris-made hats?

SORIN: Of course—of course—forgive me for momentarily forgetting what a generous, noble-hearted mother you are. I'll manage somehow to get Kostya something to wear. Shamrayev takes my entire pension, you know, and spends it on agriculture, cattle-raising. Crops fail, cattle die off— Still, I'll make your son presentable somehow.

ARKADINA: Good, do that, my son is handsome enough to be attractive in rags.

[*Sorin staggers.*]

SORIN: What's the—dizzy! —feel—dizzy . . .

ARKADINA: Petruska! [*She embraces him.*] Careful, don't fall. Help, help, somebody!

[*Enter Constantine and Medvedenko.*]

He's taken ill, all at once.

SORIN: Nothing, nothing—unusual . . .

CONSTANTINE: This often happens to Uncle now. Lie down a while, Uncle.

SORIN: Yes, just a while—going to the station all the same, don't leave without me.

MEDVEDENKO [*assisting Sorin*]: Here's a riddle for you. What goes on four legs in the morning, two legs at noon and on three in the evening?

SORIN: Yes, yes, and on the back at night . . . Thank you but I can manage alone.

MEDVEDENKO: Rest a bit first. [*He exits.*]

ARKADINA [*returning to the mirror*]: What a fright he gave me. And you know—do you like my hat? An import from Paris! I'm always photographed at the Moscow station, and it's important to my public image that I make the best possible appearance. Can I afford the hat? No! Can I afford the gown? No!

CONSTANTINE: Then how did you get them? Did you lift them from shops?

ARKADINA: Kostya!

CONSTANTINE: Mother, don't leave your poor brother forever in the hands of that despot, Shamrayev.

ARKADINA: Kostya, Shamrayev takes excellent care of my brother, and his wife is devoted to him.

CONSTANTINE: Yes, everyone loves Uncle Petrusha, or professes to, yes, and well they might! Who else but Uncle would be so concerned for me and for my—

ARKADINA: Your totally unrealistic ambition to make your way as a writer. Write! —To *amuse* yourself if you're bored here. But—Kostya, change your name and do small parts on the stage. You have the looks. I can get managers to employ you, not in big roles before you're ready for them, but—

CONSTANTINE: No! No! I'll find my way as a writer, in new forms. That I'll do or I'll—I have time, but Uncle Petrusha doesn't. He doesn't complain but he's desperate to escape for a little while to city life. If you'd stop talking such a poor mouth despite the fact we know you have a fortune! Mother, lend Uncle a couple of thousand rubles to be happy in a city. We know he's a rare person and deserves generosity from you the little while that's still left him.

ARKADINA: Please, for God's sake. I'm Russia's most prominent actress, not a banker! Aren't you proud to have a mother who's celebrated as I am?

CONSTANTINE: I'm proud of you when you forget your vanity and you're—kind . . . Will you change my bandage for me? I want to remember your tenderness before you stopped being human and turned into a famous actress.

ARKADINA: Is *that* a kind remark? Kostya, I haven't changed toward you. [*She produces a sterile solution and a box of bandages.*] The doctor's late. Never mind. Sit down. The wound's nearly healed. While I'm away, slaving on the stage to earn your keep—promise me no more click-click with that —Give it to me, that pistol! It's not safe on the place! [*A dog howls.*] *Shut up*! —Get rid of that howling dog and surrender that pistol to me before I leave.

CONSTANTINE: No, mother, don't worry. I think I've learned the lesson of control so—it won't happen again. [*She bathes his wound with disinfectant.*] You have magic fingers . . . Remember when you were playing in the state theatre? I was a child. A riot broke out among tenants in the courtyard, a wash-erwoman was badly beaten, picked up unconscious. Remember what beautiful care you took of her and her children?

ARKADINA: No, I can't, I refuse to look back on those sordid years.

CONSTANTINE: And the ballet dancers, dismissed by their company, you were so kind to them?

ARKADINA: Yes, that I do remember!

CONSTANTINE: You know, these last few days, I've felt like your son again, your child. I've no one left but you— Why have you given yourself to that—immoral man who doesn't love or respect you?

ARKADINA: *Not true!* —You don't understand Boris because you're jealous of him. He is—he has—a very noble character. Despite your attitude toward him he regards you with true con-cern, appreciation—interest!

CONSTANTINE: It's not the sort of interest that I wish to at-tract— As for his nobility— He goes swimming with Yakov—after dark . . .

ARKADINA: Which means nothing—what could it mean. Kostya, the outside world isn't an innocent world. In any case he's leaving. I'm taking him away. [*Trigorin approaches.*] The bandage isn't fastened.

CONSTANTINE: I can fasten the bandage. [*He hurries out to avoid Trigorin.*]

ARKADINA: Of course you're packing nothing. However, your things are packed.

TRIGORIN [*reading from his book*]: "If ever my life can be of use to you, come and take it."

ARKADINA: Take what?

TRIGORIN: A line I'd forgotten I'd written.

[*She snatches the book from him.*]

ARKADINA: Marked! By whom?

TRIGORIN: A very innocent native of your lake shore.

ARKADINA: You think I'm so stupid I don't know whom you mean?

TRIGORIN: Be a friend to me, Irina— Let's stay on a while.

ARKADINA: No friend to you would permit you to make such a fool of yourself.

TRIGORIN: Please, please, do let's stay!

ARKADINA: Are you so infatuated with this, this—ambitious and pretentious—creature?

TRIGORIN: A writer has needs: mine's to stay.

ARKADINA: Mine's to keep an engagement in a Moscow theatre, and I have never failed an engagement in my life.

TRIGORIN: Of course I'm not a theatrical engagement—but you're failing me— It could be the most important romance I've ever written.

ARKADINA: It's pathetic how little you know yourself— Pitiful! Pathetic! It's almost tragic!

TRIGORIN: —Let me go—Irina.

ARKADINA: —Did I hear you correctly? Did you say, "Let me go?" —*You can't talk to me like this!*

TRIGORIN: It's just that— I had no time in my youth to be young: you know that— Haunting editor's offices, accepting the insults, the crumbs, the pennies, the—

ARKADINA: Oh, yes. But I came along, didn't I? Didn't I enter your famished life, Boris, and give a sustenance to it? Tell me, yes or no? Didn't I take you to the leading publisher in Petersburg with your little collection of stories in your portfolio? Didn't I throw myself at him, didn't I shout, "I bring you GENIUS. The Tolstoy of tomorrow!" —Didn't I shout that as I snatched your portfolio from you, you young trembling nobody, and DIDN'T HE LISTEN, DIDN'T HE SIT THERE AND HEAR ME?

TRIGORIN: Yes. You were a bit—loud!

ARKADINA: Quite effectively so! —Your career was launched.

TRIGORIN: *By the volume of your voice only? By nothing in my portfolio?*

ARKADINA: HOW DARE YOU SHOUT AT ME!

TRIGORIN: We were speaking of the effectiveness of vocal volume, I thought. Is it possible I have acquired it by contagion, by constant familiarity with the thunders of Jove?

[*Pause. She draws a long and loud breath: then flings herself at his feet.*]

ARKADINA: Have I really become so old and ugly to you that you feel no shame at all in talking to me of this infatuation with this provincial goose girl?

TRIGORIN: *Stop it!* —You're speaking of someone in the—human—company of—angels . . .

[*Suddenly she changes her tactics.*]

ARKADINA: I've bruised my—afraid I've sprained my—please! Will you be so kind as to offer me some assistance in getting back on my feet?

TRIGORIN: Wouldn't it be wiser to rest on the floor a while with a pillow under your head?

ARKADINA: No—no—it would not! —I've risen without assistance! —Boris? Boris? —You're the last chapter of my life . . .

TRIGORIN: I have a feeling that with a bit of effort you might contrive to compose a heart-breaking epilogue to it somehow . . .

[*This line turns her back—silently—to rage.*]

ARKADINA: Boris—I came across something of a very curious nature while I was packing your things— A photograph enclosed in a letter from—a place abroad! Yes, Sicily! —Now why would this young correspondent, a long-haired youth, yes, a boy with great dark eyes and long lashes and—*in a bathing costume!*—address you as *"Mio Cuore"* and inscribe the enclosed photograph *"Con Amore"?*

[*Pause. Trigorin does something of a violent nature: smashes a bottle or knocks over a chair.*]

TRIGORIN: Irina, the moment has come for truth between us: there were others. Naples—Venice—Athens. Oh, not many others, but others and there was, when you met me, in the cafe in Moscow, a student who—suffered a fatal—accident, leaned too far out of the window of the room that we shared in—

ARKADINA: Boris, I am a woman of the theatre and of the world. Did you imagine that I was not aware of your perverse attraction to *what's* regarded as—*unspeakable*! —*Abomination!* But I? —Having compassion, I—

TRIGORIN: You, you, you, always you!

ARKADINA [*shouting*]: KEEP YOUR VOICE DOWN, BORIS! —These are hardly matters that you want overheard— These are my secrets as much as they are yours. And will remain my secrets as well as your secrets until the day you betray me, the day you throw me off for a girl *or* a boy that wants only to use you!

TRIGORIN: —Of course this hasn't the slightest resemblance to blackmail . . . [*He continues pacing about, breathing heavily.*] —I did not entertain prostitutes like your friend Mr. Wilde.

ARKADINA: Boris, I think you would have caught that channel boat to Calais, not waited for the police in the Hotel Cadogan, oh, I—

TRIGORIN: No. I'm not made of that stuff, I am actually a coward—morally flabby—soft—submissive. Are these characteristics you find appealing in me, Irina?

ARKADINA: Boris, I know you and I accept you and—this I swear—I love you with my whole heart.

TRIGORIN:—Then take me away from this lake— Carry me off again with you to witness your triumphs! Yes, do that, but be careful you never let me go one step away from you, ever.

ARKADINA: Nonsense. Go wherever you please and when you please, Boris. I know you'll return as well as you know I'll be waiting for you with the same unfailing devotion— You do want to remain here for a while longer? Why not? Stay! General Prokoboski will be only too happy to escort me about in Moscow.

[*Trigorin laughs silently: he regards her abruptly with understanding of her valor with its pretensions.*]

TRIGORIN: —Jealousy would consume me every night. Why, the General can't be a day over seventy! Ha ha ha . . .

[*Arkadina laughs with him, clasps him in a passionate embrace.*]

—Shameless—wanton . . . [*He releases himself gently and opens his notebook.*]

ARKADINA: Write down in your notebook, which is my only serious rival, these words: "I am adored for life by Russia's—"

TRIGORIN: —"Divine Sarah Bernhardt!" —Yes, we'll do that later— I was actually writing down a phrase that leapt into my mind from God knows where—"A grove of birches turn silver as dusk descends." So! [*He closes his notebook.*] Off again, my beloved, *madre di cuor mio*! —Railway carriages, stations, refreshment bars, warmed-over stews and—I'll hear your *Medea* and suggest—some modulated readings . . .

[*Enter Shamrayev.*]

SHAMRAYEV [*in his courtly and mock-obsequious manner*]: If I may interrupt—was it a rehearsal for your *Medea*?

TRIGORIN: Yes, it was.

ARKADINA: Now what is it? Have you come here to tell me that every four-footed animal on the place is occupied with farm work?

SHAMRAYEV: With all appropriate regret I've come to inform you that the carriage horses are at your immediate disposal, dear lady.

[*A maid brings Arkadina a cloak, etc. Enter Sorin and Medvedenko.*]

SORIN: So. Off again to new glories.

POLINA: Madam, here are some plums for the journey. I know how you hate food at station restaurants.

ARKADINA: And so it goes, returns, departures, greetings begin to lose themselves in good-byes. Life's a child's water-color, the colors all run together. All sit down for the prayer—

[*It is a Russian custom for all to sit down for prayers for a safe journey.*]

TRIGORIN [*aside*]: Excuse me, I wish for a train crash, but since it would involve others—

[*Nina becomes visible in the gathering dusk and mist on the downstage lake shore. Trigorin starts out of the interior playing area.*]

ARKADINA: Boris, where are you going?

TRIGORIN: Forgot my notebook.

ARKADINA: You just had that infernal notebook here in this room.

TRIGORIN: I've indulged myself in the purchase of a new one just in case I find time to work on—a new story. I know just where it is, it's on the bench by the lake.

ARKADINA [*as he exits*]: The notebooks multiply . . .

SHAMRAYEV: Sooner or later a writer's first notebook is exhausted. Then he gets a new one or quits writing.

ARKADINA: If that has a *double-entendre*— [*She starts to pursue Trigorin.*]

POLINA: Please, the prayer!

ARKADINA: —Yes—of course—the prayer . . . [*They sit with bowed heads again.*] —A short prayer is the sweetest to God's busy ears, dear friends. What a continual storm of human supplications he's asked to hear at all hours!

SHAMRAYEV: If you should happen to encounter the actor Suzdaltsev, Madam, will you give him—

ARKADINA: Dead for two years, and you didn't know?

[*Shamrayev crosses himself.*]

POLINA: We only receive the news you send us, Madam— Ilya, is the luggage in the carriage? —*Ilya*!

SHAMRAYEV: I was—remembering something. The tragedian Izmailov—they were in the same melodrama—he was supposed to say: "We're caught in a trap," but was drunk and came out with, "We're traught in a cap"!

POLINA: *Ilya! Luggage in carriage!* [*Shamrayev exits.*]

ARKADINA: Oh, the prayer—have we time?

POLINA: Yes, yes, the train won't leave without you.

[*They pray quietly. The light dims on them and rises on Trigorin and Nina, near the lake.*]

TRIGORIN: I saw you out here and said that you were—a notebook . . .

NINA: I did so hope you'd find a moment to see me alone once more. Boris Alekseyevich, I am leaving the lake, I am going!

[*Upstage Constantine is dimly visible, observing this scene.*]

TRIGORIN: To Moscow?

[*She nods with a slight gasp.*]

NINA: Yes, is there a chance that I can see you there?

[*Constantine closes his eyes.*]

TRIGORIN: Leaving when?

NINA: Tomorrow.

TRIGORIN: Have you—are you sure you have—money enough for the journey?

NINA: Oh, it's—not that expensive, nothing would be too expensive to—

TRIGORIN: Third class? No. Go there in style, in comfort—I make this little investment in your career on the stage—little girl . . .

NINA: No, don't!

TRIGORIN: Permit me.

[*He thrusts a number of bills lingeringly down the bodice of her white dress. Constantine's eyes open at this moment: he make a slight cry, unheard.*]

Here is— [*He scribbles in the notebook.*] —the name of a Moscow hotel.

NINA: You'll be there?

TRIGORIN: Here is where I will be. [*He continues writing.*] Molchanovka Grokholsky House. [*He tears out page and gives it to her.*] Get word to me as soon as you arrive and I will somehow find a chance to be with you at once. You understand how the world turns on—successfully practiced—duplicity?   On cunning lies?

[*She gasps and nods, unable to speak. He continues, with face contorted.*]

Then stay here!

[*Nina cries out and crouches on the bench.*]

Dear child, I meant—how can I wait till you're with me? [*He crouches beside her and kisses her repeatedly with abandon.*]

NINA: *Ahhhhhhh, ahhhhhhh! I—*

TRIGORIN: *Shhhhh.*

[*The light dims on them, rises on Arkadina.*]

ARKADINA: [*rising*]: My prayer was that we'd all meet again next summer, alive and well, especially my son, oh I'm—overcome with—here's a ruble for the three of you.

YAKOV [*aside to Cook*]: One ruble for—

COOK: Shhhh.

YAKOV: Madam Arkadina, will you remind Boris Alekseyevich that he promised me a—

ARKADINA: What *are* you talking about? Constantine! Where is he?

POLINA: Locked himself in his study, can't bear to see you leave.

ARKADINA: How like Boris to wander off for that eternal, infernal—Boris? Boris! Go ahead, get everything in the carriage.

[*She remains alone as the others exit. There is dignity and tragedy in her stoical isolation. Trigorin returns.*]

TRIGORIN: Is the departure called off again?

ARKADINA: Take me to the carriage . . . [*She takes his arm and they cross off slowly together.*] We've much to discuss privately on the train . . . [*They exit.*]

DIM OUT

ACT FOUR

It is two years later. The drawing room has now been converted into Constantine's study. Doors are indicated right and left leading to other parts of the house, and there are French doors, center, leading to the verandah. Besides the usual drawing-room furniture, there is a desk downstage left and a sofa downstage right. It is evening. The room is in semi-darkness. A single lamp with a shade is lighted. Sounds of violent weather, trees rustling, and wind howling are heard. Enter Masha and Medvedenko.

MASHA: Constantine? [*She looks around.*] Not here. The poor old man keeps asking, "Where's Kostya, where's Kostya?" He can't live without him.

MEDVEDENKO: He's afraid of being alone. I understand that.

MASHA: You're not old and sick. I think that what Pyotr Nikolayevich dreads now is being alone when he dies.

MEDVEDENKO: Such terrible weather—never seen such waves on the lake . . .

MASHA [*impatiently*]: Was that the subject?

MEDVEDENKO [*with a forlorn dignity*]: I seem unable to say a thing that doesn't annoy you.

[*She is improvising a bed for Sorin in the study.*]

MASHA: When you first spoke of the prospect of being transferred, that already annoyed me. But we're still here.

MEDVEDENKO: I have made the application for a transfer and all I can do now is wait.

MASHA: Interminably.

MEDVEDENKO: That scarf gives a touch of color to your customary black. There is a young lady who helps about the school. She said to me, "Doesn't it depress you that your wife is always in a black dress, black as a nun's habit, always?"

MASHA [*mockingly*]: Ah-ha, she's trying to disparage me in your eyes!

MEDVEDENKO: No, no, it was just an observation.

MASHA: Which you've often made yourself.

MEDVEDENKO: It is a relief at night when you discard the black dress and—your underclothes are as white as your skin.

MASHA: I always turn off the lamp when I undress.

MEDVEDENKO [*involuntarily grasping her shoulders*]: Even so— [*He can't see the revulsion on her face, but she gasps as with pain.*]

MASHA: Semyon, don't think I don't understand how little I satisfy your rational needs. Perhaps another woman—not in a nun's habit.

MEDVEDENKO: You misunderstood.

MASHA: Oh, God, did I? Constantine won't let me close the curtains on the garden. And it's so dark.

MEDVEDENKO: That stage out there by the lake, it ought to be pulled down, it stands out there so bare and ugly, now.

MASHA: A skeleton, yes, but he looks at it as if it were a portrait of Nina . . .

MEDVEDENKO: The curtains flap in the wind. Last night as I went by it I thought I heard someone crying on it.

MASHA: Probably you did—I've heard she's back.

MEDVEDENKO: Crying on the stage where she acted in Constantine's play? Masha . . .

MASHA: Please, I'm busy.

MEDVEDENKO: Have you ever given yourself to Constantine Gavrilovich?

MASHA: No. But would have! If there'd seemed a chance that he would take me.

MEDVEDENKO: If you appeared in the garden and removed the black dress and he saw the snow of—

MASHA: Stop, stop, that's disgusting. Call me black as a crow's wing but never accuse me of having *no pride left*.

MEDVEDENKO [*tearing at her dress*]: Snow, snow, but so warm. Masha, let's go home.

MASHA: I'm staying here tonight.

MEDVEDENKO: You've stayed here for three nights. Never mind if you don't mind me, but there's the baby. He's hungry.

MASHA: Matryona will feed it. Semyon, you may have to

serve as both parents to the child, and why not? It made the mistake, poor creature, of looking exactly like you and I am sure the resemblance will only increase with time. You've torn my dress. You've accused me of soliciting a young man who doesn't want me, shamelessly soliciting as a whore. Enough. Go home.

MEDVEDENKO: I don't believe you'd spend three nights here unless he'd finally accepted you, Masha.

MASHA: *Go home!*

MEDVEDENKO: Your father has no respect for me either, won't even lend me a horse.

MASHA: Walk then.

MEDVEDENKO: Don't' you mean *crawl*?

MASHA: Walk, crawl, hop! Any manner you choose to get you there—not here!

[*Enter Polina and Constantine.*]

POLINA: Poor dear Petrusha wants his bed made up for him in here.

MASHA: I know! I've made it up for him . . .

POLINA: Old people become like children.

MEDVEDENKO: Masha has refused for three nights in a row to go home to our child. Tells me I must serve as both parents to him.

POLINA: When the lake is disturbed, it seems to affect us all.

MEDVEDENKO: Constantine Gavrilovich, may I speak to you a moment in the garden?

MASHA: Leave him alone, leave everyone alone and just go.

[*Medvedenko goes out, quietly as a thief.*]

CONSTANTINE: Why did he want to speak to me in the garden?

MASHA: He wanted to warn you that I—

POLINA: Masha, your dress is torn.

MASHA: It caught on something . . .

[*Polina gives her a quick kiss and approaches Constantine at his desk.*]

POLINA: None of us thought or dreamed you'd turn out to be a recognized author. And here you are, praise God, receiving money from magazines. And you've grown so handsome, hasn't he, Masha? [*She is fingering the books on his desk.*]

MASHA: Constantine knows my—

CONSTANTINE [*to Polina*]: Please leave my books alone.

[*Something in his voice impels Masha to go out into the garden.*]

POLINA: Dear, good Kostya, will you please—

CONSTANTINE: What?

[*Masha has started back into the study.*]

POLINA: Be a little kinder to my Mashenka.

CONSTANTINE: Excuse me. [*He looks at Masha.*]

MASHA: Kostya, put on a coat, it's— [*He exits.*] Now see what you've done with that—that pitiful appeal! Embarrassed him almost as much as me. You drove him out of his study.

POLINA: Oh, you know how he wanders about, head in the clouds, he didn't hear me . . .

MASHA: Kostya's aware—everybody's aware—I can't hide it! For years before he became so obsessed by . . .

POLINA: Nina—

MASHA: —who cares only for acting, I did hope he'd want me some day. Now, never.

POLINA: *Oh, Mashenka, Mashenka! I can't bear . . .*

MASHA: Mother, you'd be surprised how many people in this world have to bear the unbearable.

POLINA: You're young, too young to—

MASHA: Observe what I observe, know what I know?

POLINA: That kind of bitterness belongs to the old and hopeless! Masha, now that he knows he's lost Nina forever to her madness, he might suddenly appreciate your devotion.

MASHA: You forget that I'm married, a mother—it's too late. My only hope is finally, at last, Semyon will be transferred somewhere so that never seeing Kostya, I'll gradually— [*A melancholy waltz fades in.*] He passes by me! I want to reach out and touch him! No, it can't continue. If Semyon gets no transfer, I'll transfer myself, somehow, somewhere . . . [*She pours herself a vodka, Polina snatches it from her.*] Thank you—I mustn't let myself go. I'll wind up a drunken prostitute on the streets.

POLINA [*taking her in her arms*]: Hush, hush.

MASHA: Sorry.

POLINA: I understand. Mashenka, I once went to Yevgeny's clinic and I—I said, "Take me, take me."

MASHA: Which he did and discarded you soon for another. Kostya's playing the piano.

POLINA: A melancholy waltz. Means he's depressed.

[*Medvedenko wheels in Sorin. They're followed by Dorn.*]

MEDVEDENKO: Six to feed in my house now and flour at two kopecks a pound. [*Dorn laughs.*] You laugh because you have more money than you know what to do with.

DORN: I live extravagantly, most of my money goes on travel and other amusements and why not? When a man dies he should know that he has lived.

MASHA: I thought surely you'd gone by now, Semyon.

MEDVEDENKO: I can't persuade your father to give me a horse of any kind—I'd take a *goat*.

MASHA [*undertone to Polina*]: How I wish I'd never set eyes on that man.

DORN: So this drawing room's been converted to a study for the new young literary master!

MASHA: And why not? Constantine needs seclusion and he likes to go out in the garden sometimes.

DORN: To meditate on the world as it will be two hundred thousand years from now, is that it?

SORIN: Where is my sister?

MASHA: Shamrayev's gone to the station to meet her and Trigorin.

[*Sorin sighs.*]

CONSTANTINE [*entering*]: Doctor Dorn, I want you to stop posing as a physician, especially as my uncle's, you just depress him!

DORN: You uncle has certain chronic, incurable—

SORIN: "Chronic, incurable" *what?* Damn it, I have a right to know.

DORN: My patients always say that but never mean it. My God, if I told them "what" they'd make such a howl and such irrational demands, why, my office would be a continual bedlam.

SORIN: But damn it, sir, how can I fight these . . . these troubles unless I know what they are. Tell what to fight and I will fight it because unreasonable as it may be, *I do want to live!*

DORN: Indefinitely, in your condition?   Forget it, old man. Every life has a beginning and an end.

SORIN: And I am at—?

DORN: *Not* at the *beginning.* [*He shrugs.*] When a man is no longer able to enjoy his sex, digest his food and sleep soundly, he's a fool to hang on.

CONSTANTINE: You are a brutal man, unfit for your profession.

DORN: As you for yours?

[*With a curse in Russian, Constantine turns away from Dorn and sits on a stool at his uncle's feet.*]

CONSTANTINE: Pay no attention to that pretentious, vicious old lecher.

[*There is an embarrassed silence in the room; the dull flash of lightning is seen through the doors onto the garden.*]

MEDVEDENKO: In your travels, Doctor, which foreign city did you like?

DORN: Any large Italian city pleases me. They're full of well-fleshed women that smile at me on the street and—

CONSTANTINE: He means whores.

DORN: Not necessarily, just women unencumbered by an excess of propriety—which reminds me—that young woman who recited that little piece of yours, she took herself seriously as an actress, you know, threw herself at your mother's famous literary friend, Trigorin, had a bastard by him before he deserted her. A sensible man gets rid of women who make themselves an insupportable nuisance. Well, it seems she's back here, staying at the Inn because her father, who's a close friend of mine, refuses to let her in his house.

[*Constantine has risen slowly to confront Dorn.*]

CONSTANTINE: A man who speaks contemptuously of a lovely girl's—tragedy—in life . . . he's not a man, he's not a human being, he's some kind of monster.

DORN [*impassively lighting a pipe or cigar*]: Ah?

CONSTANTINE: Yes, a monster. You hear me? Do you accept this definition of your nature without protest or would you like to join me in the garden with a pair of pistols?

DORN: Young man, you're insane, my medical practice is not concerned with lunacy.

MASHA: Kostya, please, please, we all know what he is, all of us despise him.

POLINA: Yes, he's not worth your attention.

ARKADINA [*offstage*]: Ah, my home!

MASHA: Your mother's arrived, she's in the hall.

DORN: The lady still has quite a powerful voice. What a pity the critics have turned against her.

ARKADINA [*offstage*]: Still dizzy from it, the triumph in Odessa.

DORN: The poor lady thinks we receive no newspapers in the provinces and are unaware that her Odessa engagement closed almost as soon as it opened.

CONSTANTINE: Can't someone drive him out? Otherwise I'll . . . I'll . . .

[*Arkadina enters; the greetings are effusive and all in Russian.*]

DORN [*after the greetings*]: Please tell us, dear lady, about your latest triumph at the Empress—was it—in Odessa?

ARKADINA: Oh, *that*! The audience simply refused to leave the theatre, remained shouting bravos an hour after the— Boris? Boris Alekseyevich?

CONSTANTINE: Mother, you look tired.

ARKADINA: It's—tiring, of course, a—career such as— mine . . .

[*She is suddenly touching: a terrified bird seems to appear momentarily in her eyes. Trigorin enters, followed by Shamrayev. There are more greetings in Russian. Constantine has returned to sit at his uncle's feet. Sorin holds Constantine's head between trembling hands.*]

Is something the matter here? You all appear so—

POLINA: Nothing at all. We're all so happy to have you back with us again.

ARKADINA: I do need a good rest. The country, the lake shore, they stay so faithfully the same . . .

TRIGORIN: And you, Masha, is it true you're married?

MASHA: Yes, for quite a while now.

TRIGORIN: Happily, I trust?

MEDVEDENKO: We have a fine little boy.

MASHA [*involuntarily*]: It's startling, the child's resemblance to its father.

[*Trigorin coughs; his eyes are on Constantine; he approaches him.*]

TRIGORIN: Constantine, your many, many admirers send their greetings to you and their felicitations along with mine on your adventurous departure from old forms to new forms that could introduce fresh new movements in the literary world. Everyone who's read your work is so excited to hear that I know you, they all want to know what you're like, your age, how you look, how you live, whether you're dark or fair. As for myself, what puzzles me is your writing under a pseudonym. Now why do you do that?

CONSTANTINE: I should think you'd understand.

TRIGORIN: Your wanting privacy, yes, but sooner or later, they'll discover the handsome young man who lives behind an iron mask.

ARKADINA: Even in this wretched weather, oh, how lucky I am to have a place to rest and to catch my breath among dear friends. Oh, Kostya! Boris has brought a magazine with your latest work in it.

TRIGORIN: Right, right, here it is, it contains your story and a story of mine.

CONSTANTINE: Which do you prefer?

ARKADINA: *Kostya*!

TRIGORIN: Naturally yours.

CONSTANTINE: Yes, the editor told me of your interest in my work.

TRIGORIN: A writer gets tired of his own work and of old forms he's been afraid to discard.

CONSTANTINE: I already have a copy of the magazine, thank you. I hope you don't think me rude but I'm not in the mood this evening for—for literary talk . . .

TRIGORIN: I, uh, understand. Another time—and you, Pyotr Nikolayevich, don't tell me you're still ailing. What I think is— you're as bored with country life as I am longing for it again.

ARKADINA: What are you doing, Polina? Ah, the lotto. How comforting to see these old familiar things. Have we time to have a game before dinner?

POLINA: Oh, a quick one.

[*Shamrayev and Polina arrange a card table and chairs. They all begin to play—except Medvedenko, and Constantine, who remains at his desk. Sounds of the game continue under the dialogue.*]

ARKADINA: The stake is five kopecks. Doctor, put mine in for me. Masha will deal. Boris!

MASHA: Have you all put down your stakes? I begin at twenty-two.

ARKADINA: I have it.

MASHA: Three.

DORN: Right.

MASHA: Did you put down three? Eight, eighty-one! Ten!

SHAMRAYEV: Not so fast.

ARKADINA: Did someone mention the Empress? The fact of the matter is— [*There is a nervous silence.*] The management and I have had strained relations for some time now. I asked to see my costumes. There were none! Schwetzoff had the audacity to pretend that I'd promised to provide my own wardrobe.

POLINA: I hope you put him in his place.

ARKADINA: I had written him that unless I was satisfied with my costumes—I would appear stark naked.

DORN: He took you up on that did he? Seriously?

ARKADINA: He took me seriously when, after three performances in my own clothes, I notified him by wire that the engagement was terminated and that I was placing the matter in the hands of my lawyer—breach of contract! He dared to threaten me with a counter suit but— [*She observes with embarrassment that no one is listening to her. She dabs her tearful eyes at the mirror.*]

MASHA: Thirty-four! Sixty! Papa, my husband must have a horse, now to get home.

SHAMRAYEV: The horses have just returned from the station and will not be disturbed again, not for the Czar himself, let alone your . . .

MASHA: You have other horses!

SHAMRAYEV: There isn't an animal on the estate that I'd send out in this weather.

POLINA: Except your daughter's husband?

MEDVEDENKO: What a fuss about nothing. It's only four miles, the walk and the weather will invigorate me . . . I hope. [*There is a thunderclap followed by lightning.*] Good night, good night all. [*He exits apologetically.*]

POLINA: Shall we continue?

MASHA: Fifty.

DORN: Exactly fifty?

ARKADINA [to Trigorin]: Have you ever been here in autumn before? The evenings are long and—lotto's a dull game but reminds me of childhood in a way that touches me so deeply . . .

TRIGORIN: When the weather's this violent it wears itself out and clear weather returns the next day.

MASHA: Seventy-seven. Eleven.

TRIGORIN: I'll probably fish tomorrow, even swim a bit since I like cold water.

CONSTANTINE: Yakov only swims in summer.

TRIGORIN: Oh? —Well . . . you know, I want to walk about the lake, have a look at the little stage where your play was performed that summer. I've started a story based on the occasion, just want to refresh my memory of the scene.

MASHA: Twenty eight!

[The last number is called.]

TRIGORIN: Ladies and gentlemen, the game is mine!

[The cook calls to Polina in Russian.]

POLINA: Cook says supper is ready, he's prepared a surprise for you, Madam, in honor of your homecoming.

ARKADINA: I do hope it's *kulebiaka.** Let's have it at once, I'm famished in the country and this time intend to indulge my

---

*A Russian meat or fish pie.

appetite—we can play another game afterwards. [*She takes the arm of Trigorin and leads them off.*] Kostya, do stop writing, at least for supper.

CONSTANTINE: If you'll excuse me, Mother, I have some notes to go over. And I'm not hungry this evening.

ARKADINA: Petrusha!

SORIN [*rousing from sleep*]: Missed it, did I? Don't tell me I missed it . . .

ARKADINA: He's still dreaming, poor soul. Wheel him to the table, please.

[*Polina and Dorn wheel out Sorin's chair as they all exit, left, leaving Constantine at the desk. Nina is just visible outside.*]

CONSTANTINE [*reading his manuscript*]: What could be more ordinary or banal?

[*The dim figure peering in makes an abrupt movement. Constantine looks up for a moment.*]

So much and no more's enough. Better nothing . . . I think I want to stop. [*Pause.*] Nina, I know you're out there! [*Her dim figure rushes away; he runs out after her. After a few moments he returns with a tight hold on her.*] Now! Stop it! [*She stares at him silently for a moment: then covers her eyes.*] Don't let's cry for God's sake. Let me take off those wet slippers. [*He removes them.*]

NINA: Turn up the lamp a little so I can see you clearly. [*He complies. They look at each other.*] Well, so it's gone, our youth.

CONSTANTINE: Not yours. [*He turns down the lamp.*]

NINA: Then why did you turn the lamp out?

CONSTANTINE: I only light it to work.

NINA: I've heard of your—success, I'm happy for you— you're not happy for yourself?

[*He shakes his head, eyes blazing with pain. She rushes to him and catches his head to her breast. He gasps and throws his arms about her. The sound of Arkadina laughing offstage is heard. Nina frees herself with a sudden, violent twist and rushes to lock the door.*]

I know Irina Nikolayevna is here. Lock the door. There's no key—

CONSTANTINE: I'll push a chair against it. [*He does so then goes to her.*] Ssshhh.

NINA: I know how much I've changed, how—different I look.

CONSTANTINE: Why wouldn't you see me? I know you've been here nearly a week. I went around the lake and stood under your window—couldn't call—just stood there like a beggar.

NINA: I've come close to this house a number of times, too— couldn't knock at the door.

[*Nina hears the sound of Trigorin laughing.*]

CONSTANTINE: "Ladies and gentlemen, the game is mine!" Who was it said that tonight when they were playing lotto before supper?

[*She nods.*]

NINA: Yes, the game is his . . .

CONSTANTINE: Why didn't he make the announcement before they played? It was already his, it would be his, and even if it weren't his he'd still assume it was his, is his, would be his in the end.

NINA: You mustn't be jealous of him.

CONSTANTINE: *You* are his.

NINA: Am I? Who does a sea gull belong to . . .

CONSTANTINE: Did you say a . . .

NINA: A sea gull. To whom does a sea gull belong? Can they feel love? It must be a thing of the moment, then flight again and even when flying together they seem to be each—alone . . .

[*The sound of the wind is heard; black, gray, and white marbled clouds appear on the backdrop. The clouds are animated; the earth seems to breathe convulsively for a moment or two.*]

There's a passage in Turgenev that goes: "Happy the man who on such a night has a roof over his head, who has a warm corner of his own." Oh, I know the Spartan requirements of an artist, how one thing after another has to be discarded, those things that are just for effect, to please vulgar tastes, such as—sentimentality—extravagances of manner. But suppose the aspiring artist divested himself of all these false adornments and underneath them found there was nothing left that his audience could see? The audience, seeing nothing, would say, "There is nothing to see."

CONSTANTINE: So you've begun to recognize that, too.

NINA: Yes, Kostya, it's the same for us both, we have to go on with this Spartan approach to—what? Not frightened by the always possible, if not probable, result of stripping off all our excesses and uncovering—finally—nothing . . . Oh, my friend, my dear friend, it's lonelier for you but don't be afraid or if you are afraid—who isn't—still go on, go on. I shall. I have future engagements to which I must travel third-class—with peasants—I am not afraid, I have no resentment left. I hold the crying children in my lap. And I cry with them.

CONSTANTINE: Nina, you're crying now.

NINA: It does me good, and what could be more natural? Being here under this roof with—

CONSTANTINE: Him.

NINA: You won't tell him? Please, no.

[*They hear the sound of Trigorin and Arkadina laughing, muted.*]

CONSTANTINE: I know you were with him a while.

NINA: Do you?

[*He nods.*]

CONSTANTINE: He treated you brutally.

NINA: It's too easy to say that. After all, remember, I did throw myself at him while he belonged to your mother. He had no commitment to me: he had to her! Oh, I'm talking falsely. Madam Arkadina is a selfish creature and he—

CONSTANTINE: Trigorin has behaved like a pig, worse, pigs are killed—he kills . . . [*Trigorin's laughter is heard.*] That's him, laughing out there. Mother must be performing a tragic death scene for him.

NINA: Hush. Remember, you're speaking of an older man who has achieved his life, his position as a fine writer . . .

CONSTANTINE: What was it like, your—

NINA: My years of attachment to him involved a child.

[*Pause.*]

CONSTANTINE: Your child and his, where is it?

NINA: The child of a sea gull is a sea gull too.

CONSTANTINE: I don't understand, where is it?

NINA: The couple to whom I—gave it when Trigorin left me—were foreigners, Kostya. By now they've returned to the other side of the world . . .

CONSTANTINE [*bitterly*]: Were they . . .

NINA: Travelers from the new world. And so my child will grow up in a new world. It has a lovely name—America . . .

CONSTANTINE: You know how to reach them to inquire sometimes—?

NINA: I have an address. Now. No more about that. Please! Today I wish to inquire . . . [*She says this with a quiet savagery, rising to catch hold of his hand. He kisses her contorted face tenderly, repeatedly.*] It if matters, let's pretend it doesn't. I have to. My years of Trigorin. He didn't believe in the theatre, only deceives your mother to please her about that, Kostya. About my dreams, my dedication to the theatre as an art, he laughed at it, regards it as a bastard profession as he regarded our child. A bastard to be given away to—travelers. Sentimentality . . . *Stop it!* . . . not so loud, they'll hear me, they mustn't know that I came here. Kostya, if you told them, you'd betray me, I'd never see you again. Allow me—pride . . .

CONSTANTINE: I allow you pride, Nina. And hope to allow it to myself, too.

NINA [*holding him close*]: I'll tell you the rest of it quickly. After the child's . . .

CONSTANTINE: Surrender . . .

NINA: Yes, there was pettiness, triviality, anxiety, envy, discoveries that shocked me. My performances were insipid, didn't know what to do with my—empty—hands, not how to stand on the stage, sometimes a cue would have to be repeated twice before I—responded— You can imagine what it's like to feel that you're acting abominably.

CONSTANTINE: Yes, I know what it's like to write abominably, Nina.

NINA [*breaking away and crossing upstage with a calm pride and stoicism*]: Let's say that a man came along by chance and, having a hunter's gun in his hand, had nothing better to do, he tried his marksmanship on a bird in the sky, a sea gull, struck home, it fell to death, fluttered a bit, then—it was still, it was very still, but *not* I! Subject for a short story.

CONSTANTINE: They say that I can only write "impressions."

NINA: Don't listen, continue, if it's your vocation, have faith that you'll achieve it. [*Again the sound of Trigorin's laughter is heard.*] It may require a certain brutality of you, things of an unpleasant nature *are* required in the pursuit of an art. *I am now an actress*! I perform with delight, not terror, I'm enraptured, not sick to death with the uncertainty of it. I act—

CONSTANTINE: Beautifully . . . you're an artist.

NINA: Not yet, but—

CONSTANTINE: You *will* be!

NINA: Who are you to decide? And who am I? We can only— go on . . . Look, Kostya, my friend. In our work what's important isn't fame, isn't glory, not those things I dreamed of which satisfy your mother. What's important? *Only to endure* . . . To be able to bear the vocation, writing or acting, never give it away like a bastard child. [*She snatches a card from a pocket.*] Mail this for me, please, don't let anyone know . . . Do you promise?

CONSTANTINE: I still say Trigorin is—

NINA: *Don't!* —Isn't it strange that I love him more than before . . . How good life used to be, here, on this side of the lake, our feelings were—delicate—as flowers . . . "Men, lions, eagles and—horned deer, geese, spiders . . . Cranes no longer wake and cry in meadows, May beetles are heard no more in the linden grove"— I have to leave now. Good-bye. Remember anything useful I may have said to you— When I'm a great actress, if ever—promise you'll come to see me. [*She starts out; he pursues her a few paces.*] No, no, don't follow me.

CONSTANTINE [*stopping, speaking as if to her*]: —You've found your way—I'm still drifting, it's—chaos . . . [*He turns back to his desk, still as if talking to her.*] I don't know why I should find it necessary to practice a profession when I have just a passing talent. [*He notices the letter she gave him.*] Just the city and country and the last names of the people. [*Silence. He tears up all his manuscripts and throws them under the desk. He exits into the garden.*]

DORN [*trying to open the door*]: It seems to be locked. [*He pushes the chair away and enters. Enter Arkadina and Polina, followed by Yakov carrying bottles, then Masha, Shamrayev, and Trigorin.*]

ARKADINA: Put the red wine on the table. Boris? Beer?

TRIGORIN: You know I've stopped drinking beer.

ARKADINA: Oh, yes, and do you know why? He wishes to preserve his elegant figure. He gained a pound and consulted a doctor who told him that beer was responsible.

TRIGORIN: I found it made me too sleepy to work.

ARKADINA: Darling! [*She plucks a hair from his gleaming black head.*] A gray hair at last.

TRIGORIN: Oh, dear me. I hope you'll lend me your dye pot.

ARKADINA [*making great eyes*]: Dye? Pot?

TRIGORIN: She's removed the label on it; it's now called Elixir. Of what? Of youth? Some day some child will take a swig of it and go into convulsions.

ARKADINA: If this is how the evening is going to continue, I'll retire at once to read.

TRIGORIN: Teasing, teasing.

ARKADINA: I'm not so sure; in fact, I've always suspected that a good deal of malice is passed off as teasing.

TRIGORIN: Dear lady.

ARKADINA: Eminent author?

TRIGORIN: Isn't it time that's our common enemy, dear? Who knows when an actress, no matter how matchless in her craft, will begin unconsciously to repeat and rely on her tricks, and who knows when a writer will either kick over the traces and write so wildly he's understood by no one but himself or fall into the easy trap of repetition, too. —Are we going to play more lotto?

ARKADINA: Haven't you noticed that I'm dealing the cards?

TRIGORIN: Lotto. A game that personifies the—

POLINA [to Yakov]: Bring in the samovar while I light the candles.

ARKADINA: Personifies the—?

TRIGORIN: The old and tedious things we do to almost persuade us that nothing has changed at all . . .

ARKADINA [stung]: —What was that you asked me at dinner? Why the Czarina didn't appear at my gala in Moscow? —I thought you knew that she doesn't know any Russian, to hold her attention I'd have to play in German.

TRIGORIN: But the Czar sent you three dozen roses? And he charged them to you?

ARKADINA: What a preposterous—

TRIGORIN: We should stop this habit of leaving open letters and bills from flower shops.

[Yakov brings in the steaming samovar, then exits. Shamrayev approaches Trigorin.]

SHAMRAYEV: Here's your sea gull exactly as you ordered, sir.

TRIGORIN: I? Ordered? A dead sea gull to be mounted? — Sorry but you're mistaken. Dead things are depressing reminders of—

ARKADINA: Then why don't you stop fishing? A caught fish is a dead fish. The cards are dealt. Boris, come and sit by me.

TRIGORIN: Oh, no, you'd peek at my cards.

ARKADINA: *What*— [*A shot is heard, offstage. Abruptly her voice alters.*] —was that? [*There is a slight pause with frightened looks exchanged.*]

DORN: —It's happened again.

ARKADINA [*dropping her cards and stumbling up from the table, upsetting a wine glass*]: *What?*

DORN: A bottle of ether exploded in my medicine kit last week and it has happened again.

ARKADINA [*only half reassured*]: *Oh, my God, I*—

DORN: Your nerves are on edge tonight. Excuse me, I'll clean up the mess, be right back. [*He exits—we see him in the garden.*] —Kostya?

ARKADINA: He hasn't come back, he said he would come right back. I'm going to— [*She starts off right. Trigorin seizes her arm.*] —What, what?

TRIGORIN: A duet? [*He dances wildly with her. Dorn returns.*]

DORN: That's all it was. These volatile liquids should be kept in metal containers . . .

[*Arkadina returns to the table.*]

DORN [*to Trigorin*]: Oh, here's that magazine that published an article from America a couple of months ago—I wanted your opinion of it . . . [*He has led Trigorin to a corner of the room.*] Get Irina away from here somehow.

[*Slight pause. Trigorin's look turns inward: he knows. Outside in the garden, lanterns flicker. Masha rises and crosses to Trigorin and Dorn. Polina follows. Irina sits rigidly alone at the table.*]

MASHA: I know that it wasn't—your ether bottle—exploding.

DORN: I suggest that—

MASHA: It's finished. Valerian drops? Isn't that the suggestion? [*A crazed laugh breaks from her. Polina draws her into her arms; she breaks away and strikes at Dorn.*] There's also the storm and the lake. Where is he?

DORN: Constantine's by the lake shore.

[*The lake scene in the background is lighted slowly as Dorn and Trigorin return to Irina alone at the lotto table. Masha and Polina move helplessly about as if under deep water.*]

Tell me, Irina, how many bows did you take at the opening night in Odessa?

TRIGORIN: A countless number.

DORN: I've never had the pleasure of seeing her taking a bow on an opening night—or closing, but have heard that they are wonderfully graceful. Irina, would you take one now?

TRIGORIN: For what occasion would she take one now?

DORN: I think the occasion is presenting itself.

[*Slowly, from far upstage two male servants are bearing Constantine's body downstage, a lantern above. Clapping a hand over her mouth, Irina now staggers up from the lotto table. She backs slowly downstage to the footlights. The audience in the theatre confronts her, as she turns about. The instinct of nearly a lifetime prevails and she bows. Her face is a tragic farewell to her profession, her life, to her deeply loved son: her victim.*]

As gracefully as that!

DIM OUT

New Directions Paperbooks—A Partial Listing

For complete listing request free catalog from
New Directions, 80 Eighth Avenue, New York 10011

†Bilingual

Aller Retour New York. NDP753.
Big Sur & The Oranges. NDP161.
The Colossus of Maroussi. NDP75.
A Devil in Paradise. NDP765.
Into the Heart of Life. NDP728.
The Smile at the Foot of the Ladder. NDP386.
Y. Mishima, *Confessions of a Mask.* NDP253.
Death in Midsummer. NDP215.
Frédéric Mistral, *The Memoirs.* NDP632.
Eugenio Montale, *It Depends.*† NDP507.
Selected Poems.† NDP193.
Paul Morand, *Fancy Goods/Open All Night.* NDP567.
Vladimir Nabokov, *Nikolai Gogol.* NDP78.
Laughter in the Dark. NDP729.
The Real Life of Sebastian Knight. NDP432.
P. Neruda, *The Captain's Verses.*† NDP345.
Residence on Earth.† NDP340.
Fully Empowered. NDP792.
New Directions in Prose & Poetry (Anthology).
Available from #17 forward to #55.
Robert Nichols, *Arrival.* NDP437.
J. F. Nims, *The Six-Cornered Snowflake.* NDP700.
Charles Olson, *Selected Writings.* NDP231.
Toby Olson, *The Life of Jesus.* NDP417.
George Oppen, *Collected Poems.* NDP418.
István Örkeny, *The Flower Show/*
The Toth Family. NDP536.
Wilfred Owen, *Collected Poems.* NDP210.
José Emilio Pacheco, *Battles in the Desert.* NDP637.
Selected Poems.† NDP638.
Michael Palmer, *At Passages.* NDP803.
Nicanor Parra, *Antipoems: New & Selected.* NDP603.
Boris Pasternak, *Safe Conduct.* NDP77.
Kenneth Patchen, *Because It Is.* NDP83.
Collected Poems. NDP284.
Selected Poems. NDP160.
Ota Pavel, *How I Came to Know Fish.* NDP713.
Octavio Paz, *Collected Poems.* NDP719.
A Draft of Shadows.† NDP489.
Selected Poems. NDP574.
Sunstone.† NDP735.
A Tale of Two Gardens. NDP841.
A Tree Within.† NDP661.
Victor Pelevin, *The Yellow Arrow.* NDP845.
Ezra Pound, *ABC of Reading.* NDP89.
The Cantos. NDP824.
Confucius. NDP285.
Confucius to Cummings. (Anth.) NDP126.
Diptych Rome-London. NDP783.
Elektra. NDP683.
Guide to Kulchur. NDP257.
Literary Essays. NDP250.
Personae. NDP697.
Selected Cantos. NDP304.
Selected Poems. NDP66.
Caradog Prichard, *One Moonlit Night.* NDP835.
Eça de Queirós, *Illustrious House of Ramires.* NDP785.
Raymond Queneau, *The Blue Flowers.* NDP595.
Exercises in Style. NDP513.
Mary de Rachewiltz, *Ezra Pound.* NDP405.
Raja Rao, *Kanthapura.* NDP224.
Herbert Read, *The Green Child.* NDP208.
P. Reverdy, *Selected Poems.*† NDP346.
Kenneth Rexroth, *An Autobiographical Novel.* NDP725.
Classics Revisited. NDP621.
More Classics Revisited. NDP668.
Flower Wreath Hill. NDP724.
100 Poems from the Chinese. NDP192.
100 Poems from the Japanese.† NDP147.
Selected Poems. NDP581.
Women Poets of China. NDP528.
Women Poets of Japan. NDP527.
Rainer Maria Rilke, *Poems from*
The Book of Hours. NDP408.
Possibility of Being. (Poems). NDP436.
Where Silence Reigns. (Prose). NDP464.
Arthur Rimbaud, *Illuminations.*† NDP56.
Season in Hell & Drunken Boat.† NDP97.

Edouard Roditi, *Delights of Turkey.* NDP445.
Jerome Rothenberg, *Khurbn.* NDP679.
Seedings & Others Poems. NDP828.
Nayantara Sahgal, *Rich Like Us.* NDP665.
Ihara Saikaku, *The Life of an Amorous Woman.*
NDP270.
St. John of the Cross, *Poems.*† NDP341.
William Saroyan, *Fresno Stories.* NDP793.
Jean-Paul Sartre, *Nausea.* NDP82.
The Wall (Intimacy). NDP272.
P. D. Scott, *Crossing Borders.* NDP796.
Listening to the Candle. NDP747.
Delmore Schwartz, *Selected Poems.* NDP241.
In Dreams Begin Responsibilities. NDP454.
Hasan Shah, *The Dancing Girl.* NDP777.
C. H. Sisson, *Selected Poems.* NDP826.
Stevie Smith, *Collected Poems.* NDP562.
Novel on Yellow Paper. NDP778.
A Very Pleasant Evening. NDP804.
Gary Snyder, *The Back Country.* NDP249.
Turtle Island. NDP381.
Gustaf Sobin, *Breaths' Burials.* NDP781.
Muriel Spark, *The Comforters.* NDP796.
The Driver's Seat. NDP786.
The Public Image. NDP767.
Enid Starkie, *Rimbaud.* NDP254.
Stendhal, *Three Italian Chronicles.* NDP704.
Antonio Tabucchi, *Pereira Declares.* NDP848.
Nathaniel Tarn, *Lyrics . . . Bride of God.* NDP391.
Dylan Thomas, *Adventures in Skin Trade.* NDP183.
A Child's Christmas in Wales. NDP812.
Collected Poems 1934–1952. NDP316.
Collected Stories. NDP626.
Portrait of the Artist as a Young Dog. NDP51.
Quite Early One Morning. NDP90.
Under Milk Wood. NDP73.
Tian Wen: *A Chinese Book of Origins.* NDP624.
Uwe Timm, *The Snake Tree.* NDP686.
Lionel Trilling, *E. M. Forster.* NDP189.
Tu Fu, *Selected Poems.* NDP675.
N. Tucci, *The Rain Came Last.* NDP688.
Paul Valéry, *Selected Writings.*† NDP184.
Elio Vittorini, *A Vittorini Omnibus.* NDP366.
Rosmarie Waldrop, *A Key into the Language of America.*
NDP798.
Robert Penn Warren, *At Heaven's Gate.* NDP588.
Eliot Weinberger, *Outside Stories.* NDP751.
Nathanael West, *Miss Lonelyhearts &*
Day of the Locust. NDP125.
J. Wheelwright, *Collected Poems.* NDP544.
Tennessee Williams, *Baby Doll.* NDP714.
Cat on a Hot Tin Roof. NDP398.
Collected Stories. NDP784.
The Glass Menagerie. NDP218.
Hard Candy. NDP225.
A Lovely Sunday for Creve Coeur. NDP497.
The Roman Spring of Mrs. Stone. NDP770.
Something Cloudy, Something Clear. NDP829.
A Streetcar Named Desire. NDP501.
Sweet Bird of Youth. NDP409.
Twenty-Seven Wagons Full of Cotton. NDP217.
Vieux Carre. NDP482.
William Carlos Williams, *Asphodel.* NDP794.
The Autobiography. NDP223.
Collected Poems: Vol. I. NDP730.
Collected Poems: Vol. II. NDP731.
The Collected Stories. NDP817.
The Doctor Stories. NDP585.
Imaginations. NDP329.
In The American Grain. NDP53.
In The Money. NDP240.
Paterson. NDP806.
Pictures from Brueghel. NDP118.
Selected Poems (new ed.). NDP602.
Wisdom Books:
St. Francis. NDP477; *Taoists.* NDP509;
Wisdom of the Desert. NDP295.
Yūko Tsushima, *The Shooting Gallery.* NDP846.

For complete listing request free catalog from
New Directions, 80 Eighth Avenue, New York 10011   †Bilingual